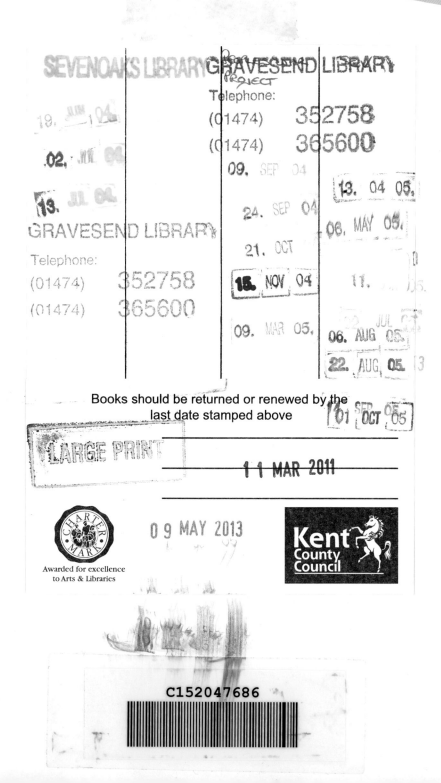

THE SOLDIER'S WIFE

Also available in this series:

Christian Anderson	THE ELEPHANT'S CHILD
Fred Archer	THE VILLAGE OF MY CHILDHOOD
Adrian Bell	CORDUROY
	SILVER LEY
	THE CHERRY TREE
Derek Brock	GLORIOUS POVERTY
Mary Sydney Burke	THE SOLDIER'S WIFE
Joyce Dennys	AND THEN THERE WAS ONE
Richard van Emden	VETERANS: THE LAST SURVIVORS OF
and Steve Humphries	THE GREAT WAR
Jean Faley	UP OOR CLOSE
Anne Garnett	CAUGHT FROM TIME
Ken Hankins	A CHILD OF THE THIRTIES
Gregory Holyoake	THE PREFAB KID
Erma Harvey James	WITH MAGIC IN MY EYES
Brian P. Martin	TALES OF THE OLD COUNTRYWOMEN
	TALES FROM THE COUNTRY PUB
Roger Mason	GRANNY'S VILLAGE
Katherine Moore	QUEEN VICTORIA IS VERY ILL
J. Morris and P. Morgan	THROUGH THE CLASSROOM WINDOW
Humphrey Phelps	UNCLE GEORGE AND COMPANY
Tom Quinn	TALES OF THE OLD COUNTRY
	FARMERS
Robert Roberts	A RAGGED SCHOOLING
Walter Rose	GOOD NEIGHBOURS
Elizabeth Seager	"THE COUNTRYMAN" BOOK OF
	VILLAGE TRADES AND CRAFTS
Edward Storey	LETTERS FROM THE FENS
C. Henry Warren	THE HAPPY COUNTRYMAN
	ADAM WAS A PLOUGHMAN
Elizabeth West	HOVEL IN THE HILLS

THE SOLDIER'S WIFE

WIFE

Peace and War

MARY SYDNEY BURKE

ISIS
LARGE PRINT
Oxford and Orlando

First published in Great Britain 1999
by Janus Publishing Company Ltd

Published in Large Print 2000 by ISIS Publishing Ltd,
7 Centremead, Osney Mead, Oxford OX2 0ES, and
ISIS Publishing, PO Box 195758,
Winter Springs, Florida 32719-5758, USA
by arrangement with Janus Publishing Company Ltd

British Library Cataloguing in Publication Data
Burke, Mary Sydney
    The soldier's wife. – Large print ed.
    1. Burke, Mary Sydney – Family 2. Army spouses – Great
    Britain – Biography 3. World War, 1939-1945 – Personal
    narratives, British 4. World War, 1939-1945 – Women –
    England 5. Large type books
    I. Title
    940.5'3'082'0941

ISBN 0-7531-5725-X (hb)
ISBN 0-7531-5746-2 (pb)

Printed and bound by Antony Rowe, Chippenham and Reading

I dedicate this book to my
four children,
Josephine, Kevin, Roberta and Bernard

CONTENTS

Foreword by Alan R. Stockdale. MLA

Treasurer of Victoria
Minister for Multimedia
Member for Brighton

Mary Burke's "The Soldier's Wife" is a story of a woman's life of the family and other people who interact with the author and the impact of world war on Mary and her family.

This is a story which goes beyond the great political and social events of the twentieth century to chronicle their impact on the life of a strong, independent woman. Mary Burke's early childhood in England is one of a warm, supportive family life and of well-remembered travels which, perhaps, led to her refuge in travel as her adult and married life became more difficult.

As the title of this chronicle suggests, much of the book concerns her marriage. Her's is a marriage for much of which the army is the context which imposes responsibility to be both father and mother on Mary as training and then active service takes her husband away from Mary and their children.

Her married life was not an easy or comfortable one. Her husband, Joe, is a difficult partner. Following the war, he is diagnosed as a schizophrenic, prone to violent outbursts leading to abuse of his wife. She is largely left to cope on her own for long periods in Singapore. This is a period of her life she describes in rich detail, revealing, in particular, her delight with her entry into retail fashion. In Australia, despite Mary's success as a couturier, Joe's inability to manage money faces the family with debts which deprive Mary of the financial rewards of her own hard work.

The book frankly, and sometimes with abundant passion, describes the joy of Mary's good times and the pain of bad times. Perhaps a shared solace in Joe's passion for music, Mary's strong support for her husband, Joe, and, especially, the strength of Mary's Catholic faith explain her lifelong ability to carry on, with courage and dignity, even in adversity.

Whether describing her early life in England, the life of a soldier's wife in Singapore, an unhappy return to England or emigrating to Australia, Mary Burke records her life and her shared life with Joe with charm and the precise word-pictures of a keen and thoughtful observer. This is a personal chronicle: life in England at war; three years in Singapore and then emigration to Australia. The personal nature of the chronicle, the strength and personal honesty of the description, makes the book both interesting and an important contribution to a more personal form of history than is offered by more academic tomes.

Widowed in 1981, Mary Burke still lives in Australia. She continues to hold to her creed that it is important to grasp happy times when they come and to enjoy them to the full.

PART ONE

England, World War Two

CHAPTER ONE

The Calm Before the Storm

Imagine the tranquillity of an English garden, a few years before the lowering clouds of World War Two descended in angry form.

Sense the stillness of a June evening whilst lazily reclining on the freshly cut lawn. I watched the clouds drifting towards the night sky, a perfused breeze fanned the tall elm trees which shielded our red-brick cottage from a narrow country lane. It all seemed too beautiful to last.

My eyes wandered to the front path, bordered on either side with roses of all colours and fragrances. Sweet Allison at the edge with tall hollyhocks, and lupine in the background. Rambler roses provided shade for the front door and lilies surrounded the bay window,

The thrush had just finished his song when the nightingale, perched high in the elderberry tree, began his tuneful notes.

The evening was so perfect that I began to feel restless, knowing that it would not last forever.

My sister and I — Amy and Mary, respectively — had spent our childhood roaming the fields of buttercups and cowslips behind our long back garden where Faith, Hope, and Charity stood — the three tall elm trees. We had named them ourselves. In summer, their leafy branches spread far and wide. In winter they stood bare and grotesque.

From our bedroom windows we watched the cuckoo perched on the apple tree. He would cuckoo so often that the sound would become monotonous until his note shortened to "cuck", as if he were tired, and then he would fly away until next year.

My father, who tended the garden, loved all the birds, especially the one-legged robin redbreast who returned every winter to perch on father's fork, waiting for worms to appear.

There was the frog who would show up at the kitchen door, and thrushes that laid their eggs in the bushes nearby.

As children, we paddled in the brook that skirted the end of the lane; we fed the donkeys and picked the wild celandines.

My sister, who was two years younger than me, had blonde hair, blue eyes, and pink cheeks. I was tall and slim, with chestnut red hair and brown eyes. My hair was always cut short but had an upward curl.

When the snow fell against the windows, we would rush out joyously in our warm coats, throw snowballs and make a snowman.

The gossamer webs of the spiders gleamed in the winter sun. Inside the house, log fires burned to warm our frozen fingers.

Spring came, and snowdrops appeared in the frozen ground, then the primroses, bluebells and leaves burst into life with the first radiance of sunlight.

Chestnut trees raised their fluffy pink and white candle-shaped blossom, and the cycle of life was re-enacted. My mother called me in from the garden; there was a meal, and later a comfortable bed and an alarm clock to set for six o'clock the next morning, my school years now over. I had to be ready for my job at the fashion house in the West End of London after completing my training in dressmaking and design at the Technical College in Barrett Street.

There was a daily half-hour walk to the railway station at Eastcote to catch the 7.30 train, taking me to London.

There was still an enormous amount to learn, but I loved handling the priceless materials, and helping to make the long white gowns worn by the debutantes at the Court of King George VI.

The head-dress always consisted of the Prince of Wales Feathers — three ostrich feathers mounted on a band and situated on the centre of the forehead. Many of our clients were titled people, not excluding royalty.

In those days, a working man's wage ranged from three pounds per week to six pounds. My pay was 30 shillings a week and was supposed to be enough to provide train fares, lunches, food and clothing.

I saved quite a lot of money by making my own dresses and suits out of my mother's "hand-me downs", using the latest Paris styles. Once I made three summer frocks out of nine yards of gingham at sixpence a yard. There was enough over for hats to match — a trade I had learned from my mother, who had made hats for the upper crust of London. She was often nicknamed the "Duchess of Devonshire" for her smart appearance.

My father, 20 years her senior, had a youthful skin, fresh complexion and pure white hair. He retired early from work and became a local councillor. He loved England so that, although he had travelled widely in Europe in his youth, the English countryside and historic places of London were his greatest delight. He enjoyed showing my sister and me the treasures of the National and Tate Art Galleries, the Royal Academy, the Victoria and Albert Museum, and the Old Chelsea Pensioners' Home, which had been built for the mistress of King Charles the First — Nell Gwyn, the orange seller. It is said there is a secret underground passage directly connecting it to Buckingham Palace. The Houses of Parliament and Westminster Abbey were other delights.

In remembering the summer holidays from school, such time was spent exploring Scotland after travelling all night on the Flying Scotsman or the Royal Scot. We stayed in Dunoon for the Gathering of the Clans and watched a thousand bagpipers playing the pipes on the hills.

The sea trip around the west coast of Scotland to Ayr was one of the roughest I can remember, but my father walked with us on deck and gave us fruit sweets to suck — his cure for seasickness. "Keep the saliva working and keep warm" was his remedy, and to this day, although I have sailed around the world many times, I have never been sick at sea.

Another year we travelled by train to Oban, visited the burial ground of the Scottish Kings in Staffa and Iona (a bleak island off the west coast), and Fingal's Cave. We took a boat up the Caledonian Canal to Invemess, passing Fort William and Fort Augustus, the eight locks taking us up to Loch Ness and finally to the Firth of Forth and Inverness. We visited the battle ground of Culloden, where the English fought the Scots many years ago.

Whilst we were still teenagers we had the pleasure of seeing Wales, climbing Snowdon by train, visiting Festiniog and Llanfairfechan. Another year it was Ireland, Waterford, Cork and Galway Bay. We walked miles through the Gap of Dunloe to a waiting rowing boat, where we had the added thrill of shooting the rapids and were told Irish legends by the old man operating the boat until we arrived in Killarney.

My favourite memory of Ireland was of Galway Bay by moonlight, with the mountains of Connemara in the background.

One day we took a boat from Galway across the rough waters of the Atlantic to the Isle of Arran, where live a swarthy breed of Irish men and women, some direct descendants of the Spaniards cast ashore from the Spanish Armada.

Their features were dark skinned, with high cheekbones, and lined from the hard work of carrying seaweed from the shore to their rockbound island to enrich the turf on which to grow the praties.

As our cargo boat approached the quay with its odorous cargo of goats, we noticed that all the young boys were dressed in long coarsely woven skirts, handwoven by the women, with wide leather belts. The men spent their time fishing in boats they had made themselves from skins of animals, and then smeared with tar. The lightness of the boats enabled them to be carried on the back after a day's fishing. The boat was called a coracle.

On one occasion we stayed in Dublin with friends of my father. The hospitality of the Irish has to be seen to be believed. One friend owned a grocery shop in Rathcoole; he had nine children. When they were hungry they would simply help themselves here and there. I never heard what became of the business or if any profit was made. Our friend insisted that we stay for tea with other friends who had dropped in unexpectedly. There were twenty-five people sitting down to high tea that day.

Then we were entreated to stay a week, in fact not allowed to refuse. After rides in the jaunting car (a horse carriage with seats either side), we arrived home without lights in the late evening, in spite of the fact they lived opposite the police station. Sure! — you never worry in Ireland.

One of the daughters of the family had joined the enclosed Order of Carmelite nuns. She had just made her final vows and we were allowed to go and visit her, so next day we took off in a convoy of cars of doubtful descriptions.

Our friend knocked on the convent door. It was soon opened as if by remote control. A voice said, "Take the door on the right." We all piled into a room, part of which was barred and shuttered. Soon the shutters opened and a young nun appeared, radiantly beautiful, smiling happily. She contrasted sharply with the sad faces of her mother and father, sisters and brothers. She told us of her happiness and showed us the white wedding gown she had worn whilst taking her vows.

After the meeting we were led into the chapel, where there was the sound of angels singing; the nuns were chanting behind the grille. We felt the tears come into our eyes as we heard their sweet, pure voices.

Our next Dublin visit was to another friend of my father, a Director of Irish Railways, where we were treated to the utmost in Dublin hospitality. With Irish impetuosity he insisted on circling the round dining table to make sure that we had everything just right, at the same time expounding the theories of the Sinn Fein movement — meaning "Ourselves Alone".

He declared that he did not agree with our politics — but he could not do enough to please us, even getting us tickets for the famous Abbey Theatre, where all the best plays have had their origin, and taking us to see a play.

All these childhood trips seem to have whetted my appetite for travel in a way that no number of ensuing years could quench.

CHAPTER
TWO

Hints of War

There was an unusual influx of German maids or "au pair" girls into Britain as the larger English homes lost their status symbols, the maids, butlers and chauffeurs, to other occupations. We were told that it was to learn the language, but looking back, with Germany re-arming, we often thought quite a lot of espionage went on at that time.

However, fares to the Continent were low. I had saved a little money from my wages, now at the enormous sum of three pounds per week. Consequently, in June 1937 I deserted my sewing job and obtained the position of governess to the two children of a prominent French family, who owned the Chateau Agny, near Arras in the north of France. The Chateau had belonged to the former Mayor of Arras. It was surrounded by a large estate and it was to be a short summer holiday job. I would teach the children English, at the same time hoping to gain a little experience of life abroad. It was also the year of the Paris Exhibition, which I hoped to be able to visit.

A few weeks before leaving England, Joe had come into my life; a handsome six-foot-three regular soldier in the Grenadier Guards. He had visited my home and we were on friendly terms. He had vowed to be true to me, writing in my autograph book the following words: "I don't want to be merely a friend — but to be with you right to the end". There were many things to do before settling down. I said a loving goodbye to my parents and new boyfriend and was soon on my way across the English Channel on my first European adventure at the age of 17.

On arrival at Arras I was given a note by the stationmaster to say that Madame had gone home as the train was late, and that I was to take a taxi. Meanwhile I was being greeted by an English gentleman who demanded that I must meet the Major; but on seeing the Major, it turned out to be a case of mistaken identity, which I had suspected anyway. I followed the instructions and took a taxi to the Chateau Agny.

After a long ride through the French countryside the taxi turned sharply to the left. Two large wrought iron gates opened into a driveway to the old Chateau.

Madame was there to greet me with Caroline and Shupette, the two children — seven and ten years of age. I was shown through the Chateau with its thick walls and heavy furniture.

My room looked out onto a lake. My bed was of solid mahogany with spotless linen and continental down quilt.

The children were very mischievous at dinner, which began at eight o'clock and lasted until nearly ten. They drank wine with their meal, which consisted of soup or delicious hors-d'oeuvres, stewed partridge complete with head, and vegetables. Fruit or cheese was to follow.

Madame, too, became highly excited after drinking some of their home-pressed cider. She would prance around the table shouting, "My husband, he is a thief, he stole my dowry."

Happily, Monsieur — a calm and tolerant man — was quite used to these outbursts. He would point to his head to indicate to me that this was not unusual. She was slightly inebriated and he was not unduly worried.

Monsieur spent many hours roaming the large estate with his gun and would return with a bird or a rabbit. Some mornings were spent cleaning the gun, with every part laid out over the breakfast room table. I then kept well out of the way.

There were two dogs tied up outside their respective kennels at each end of the Chateau. They barked at the slightest noise. The back of the Chateau was faced by a conservatory looking out onto a field, where a few sickly cows and a horse with its ribs almost protruding, nibbled the grass.

Every day church bells tolled mournfully for some recently departed soul and Madame would appear in a smart black suit, small hat to match, complete with veil, and cheerfully announce that she was off to visit the bereaved. This happened quite often; I began to think that she really enjoyed it.

My days were spent knitting and sewing. At one stage I was asked to make Monsieur a pair of pyjamas, for which he had to be duly fitted by his wife. When she found me knitting, it was suggested that I make her a woollen jacket.

There were the English lessons and walks around the wooded estate. We were always searching under the trees for some delicacy. I never really discovered what it was we were looking for, but I guess it must have been truffles. We never found any.

On one of my days off I was told I must visit the Art Gallery in Arras.

It was a cold weekday morning as I waited for the bus, which soon trundled into view. I found a seat and began to survey the scene. It was full of plump, dark women and swarthy men with lined faces. The women were enveloped in lumpy dark shawls and carried large baskets, from whence there was an occasional flutter of wings. A live chicken or duck would poke his head out. The people chattered, and garlic was the perfume of the day.

We arrived in Arras after a bumpy ride along the cobble-stoned streets. On entering the modern white building of the Art Gallery, I found that I was the only visitor and so was allocated a uniformed guide, a short Frenchman with a small moustache. He invited me into each salon, lined with enormous paintings, all of nude women floating on clouds of chiffon, and as I stopped to admire each work of art he declared in a bored voice, "Toute le même" (all the same).

In the final room, he slyly closed the door, placed an arm around me and pointed to the view from the window. I quickly withdrew and was out of the door and down the marble staircase before he had time to adjust his cap, but I unfortunately took the wrong door and ended up in a room full of male civil servants.

Thirty Frenchmen whose heads had been buried in their respective writings were now staring and giggling at the nervous English girl standing in the doorway of the Municipal Office.

My next jaunt was by train to the famous Paris Exhibition of 1937. Monsieur drove me to the Gare d'Arras and escorted me to the train for Paris. I seated myself in a carriage where everyone was talking excitedly In French. They smiled at me, but I had to remain silent as their speech was too fast to follow.

I thought I looked very smart in the new grey suit and velvet hat that I had made myself, but on reflection I must have looked very drab, except, perhaps, for my red hair.

As it was a Sunday, on arriving at the Gare du Nord I made straight for the nearest gendarme, showing him a picture of the Sacré-Coeur de Montmartre, where I wanted to attend Mass. I was directed to a tram which was divided into three parts; first, second, and those who clung to the rear.

Knowing my dilemma, all the people in the tram wanted to come to my aid, so that I was duly despatched at my destination.

I climbed the steep steps to the enormous front door of the basilica and entered. During Mass I was amused to hear the sound of a procession moving up the aisle for the giving, or collection.

A man clothed in a military-style uniform complete with gold epaulettes and large tricome hat thumped a large stick on the floor to announce the approach of the bearer of the collection bag, which was passed along each row of seats on a long pole.

Mass proceeded to its conclusion, aided by a fine choir, and I was able to leave the church and to contemplate the wonderful view over Paris from the summit of the hill of Montmartre.

The Exhibition seemed to occupy the whole of the Champs-Elysées and the surrounds of the Eiffel Tower. I walked for miles, taking in the numerous pavilions, including the stark grandeur of the German pavilion, which confronted the Russian pavilion on the opposite side of the Champs-Elysées.

I remember seeing some German officers greeting each other with the Hitler salute.

I tasted the various dishes in the Scandinavian restaurants, joined a queue and found myself in a news cinema, then rested my aching feet by the fountains of the Trocadero.

As the day closed and the lights began to twinkle, the illuminations were switched on. The Eiffel Tower and its surroundings became a fairyland.

I was alone in Paris at the age of 17 without a fear in the world, and as the fireworks began to spread over the night sky, I had to run to catch the train back to Arras, where Monsieur had arranged to pick me up and drive me back to the Chateau. My Grenadier boyfriend, by now tired of waiting for my return to England, sent me the return fare, which I stubbornly sent back until I could afford to pay it myself. The time eventually arrived for me to return home. I had overrun my holiday by several weeks but had gained much in experience.

The day arrived for me to say farewell to my French friends amid tears from the children and entreaties to stay longer. There was a strange request from Monsieur to carry a basket of pigeons to England, but as I had more luggage than I could handle, I had to refuse.

CHAPTER
THREE

The Gathering Storm

The fashion house where I was employed as a dressmaker was a relic of the past grandeur of London and was situated in Grosvenor Street, a few doors from New Bond Street in the West End.

Four pillars marked the entrance, with steps ascending to two impressive glass doors which, when opened, led to a large showroom which glowed softly from lighted wall brackets and a very large crystal chandelier hanging from the ceiling.

The showroom, with its thickly carpeted air of gentility and the fragrance of expensive perfume, was attended by young vendeuses in well-cut teal-coloured dresses, ready to serve the clients who arrived, mostly by appointment, to consult with the High Priest of fashion — Victor Stiebel. Behind the showroom were offices and upstairs were our workrooms, which in the old days had served as bedrooms, still with large mirrors on the marble mantelpieces.

The ironing was done in the bathroom, which was completely lined with mirrors from top to bottom.

The girls arrived by the back door, which led on to the mews where once horses and carriages were housed.

Now an occasional Roll-Royce was seen, complete with uniformed chauffeur.

Our fitter, a petite Frenchwoman, quiet and efficient, handled the girls well, provided they did their sewing to her satisfaction, for the clients were paying anything from £300, which was a lot of money in those days for a model gown.

My pay had now soared to three pounds, five shillings per week, but this still had to be divided into train fares, living expenses, clothes and holidays.

My Grenadier Guard friend was a constant visitor to my home at weekends or when his leave passes permitted. We would cycle or walk in the country. I had also joined the London Polytechnic Rambling Club in Regent Street, where students of all nationalities could meet each other. We visited places of interest in London or would go for ten-mile walks into the English countryside. Saturday nights were always dance nights. My sister had joined the fencing club and we both made many good friends.

People in England were fully aware of the upsurge of the Nazi Party in Germany and their rearmament programme. My mother often declared that there would be another war, but the media constantly obliterated any mention of the subject.

We listened to the radio and heard the maniacal outbursts of Hitler and his mad obsession to rid Germany of its Jewish population. We saw news films at our local cinema of Stormtroopers goose-stepping through Berlin, arms raised in the Nazi salute. We saw Goebbels grovelling to Hitler and filling the world with lies and propaganda. We saw the obese figure of Goering, his chest smothered with medals, some of which were unjustly acquired.

Maybe because of the uncertainty of approaching doom, holidays in Europe were at their lowest rate ever.

My sister suggested that we take a chance and have a holiday in Biarritz in the south of France, so we then selected a travel agent. This was the last time we were to be together, as our paths were to take completely different directions.

In June 1939 we crossed the English Channel by boat and took the night train from Paris to Biarritz, stopping only at Bayonne early next morning for coffee and croissants. Arriving at our destination, we found our hotel in an opera-like setting on the rugged coast of the Bay of Biscay.

The Bay was misty pink with hydrangeas and pale green with tamarisk trees, and our hotel faced grassy lawns laid out around the bandstand. Tired out after a sleepless night on the train, we went to bed early and were wakened in the evening by sounds of music and gaiety. People seemed to be singing and laughing in the square outside the hotel.

"Come on," I urged my sister, "we mustn't miss a thing." So we dressed and went down to evening dinner.

People were gathered around the doorway laughing and talking. "It's Fiesta," they replied to our inquiries. At that moment I became aware of two gorgeous brown eyes turned in my direction.

He was tall with olive skin; a good-looking young Frenchman. He wasted no time in coming to my side, and introduced himself as the son of the proprietress of the hotel, a dignified lady dressed in black silk. He proceeded to describe the events that would take place.

It was the custom to parade the effigy of a bull around the square. Fireworks had been inserted into the body of the bull and would be let off later in the evening. The bandstand was decorated with hundreds of Chinese lanterns and the band began to play dance music.

He led me into the square, took my arm gently, and we began to sway to the rhythm of the tango. We danced together under the starlit sky until well after midnight, then a light rain began to fall; the Chinese lanterns began popping out one by one.

Soon, a tall good-looking brother of my handsome partner came out of the hotel carrying a white raincoat, which was tenderly placed on my shoulders.

We walked slowly back to the shelter of the hotel, too tired to talk but very happy with a promise from Antoine to take my sister and I surf bathing the following day, He only spoke a little English and I a little French, but we seemed to communicate very well.

Next day we lay in the sun, bathed in the sea and ate ice cream on the terrace. My sister had meanwhile met some Welsh people, so we all went to play pelota — the national game of the Basques. We attached the long wicker basket tube to our arms and tossed the balls forward against the wall.

One of my greatest wishes was fulfilled on the next day of our holiday. We took a coach to Lourdes, to the shrine where Saint Bernadette had seen the vision of the Blessed Virgin Mary.

We passed through valleys of the Pyrenees mountains until we arrived at the Grotto by the River Gave. We knelt at the Grotto where Our Lady's statue is placed, surrounded by lighted candles. There were hundreds of crutches left behind by those who had been cured.

We filled bottles of water from the spring and then went to visit the three churches built one on top of the other, fulfilling the request of the Virgin Mary to Bernadette. We then explored the surroundings of the Grotto, where we rubbed shoulders with the late film star Tyrone Power and a companion.

There was a man on the coach on the way to Lourdes with very outspoken views on Communism, expounding his atheistic theories with a great deal of enthusiasm, but on the way back he was very quiet. I wonder: did a miracle take place that day?

Two days later there was a tour of the Pyrenees to a mountain named La Rhune, where we took a train to the summit and could see for miles into Spain. With one foot in Spain and one in the Basque country, we gazed out at the once war-torn, now apparently peaceful, land.

We arrived back at the hotel to a beautifully cooked dinner. My friend, Antoine, shyly greeted me and after dinner entreated me to prolong my holiday as there was a bullfight the following week. But all good things come to an end and money was running out fairly rapidly.

I was tempted to stay, but war clouds were looming and there was a little French girl who had her eye on him, so we reluctantly decided to say "au revoir" to our French friends and take the train back to Paris and finally England, after a madly wonderful holiday in Europe.

CHAPTER FOUR

War Declared

When life seemed at its rosiest, the painful news hit the headlines that Neville Chamberlain, the Prime Minister, had failed in his attempt to procure peace. The agreement promising peace, signed by Hitler, was worthless.

German troops had marched into Poland. Consequently England was at war with Germany and eight months later Winston Churchill became our new Prime Minister. From that moment the world was changed. We turned on our radio sets as Churchill entreated us to gird our loins for the hard times ahead, inspiring us to take courage. With the help of God, he exhorted, we would fight in the air, in the sea, and on the beaches, and never surrender.

No sooner had war broken out than the first grim reminder wailed out its agonising warning; the air raid siren to which we were all to become so accustomed.

My mother and grandmother took a cushion and sat under the stairs. They had already had experience of World War One. We listened for the sound of planes, but could hear nothing save the birds and the autumn breeze fanning the elderberry tree outside the front door. After

20 minutes the "All Clear" sounded its more even tone of relief. The pattern of our lives changed dramatically.

Visits from my Grenadier, namely Joe and now a corporal, became less frequent. The resplendent uniform of scarlet and blue was now discarded for the battle dress of a soldier at war. It now meant that he would be away for long periods of intensive training.

There were gas masks to be collected, together with ration books and clothing coupons. Long queues became the order of the day.

Young men seemed to disappear off the face of the earth. There were no more dances at the Polytechnic Club.

There was no time for a romantic proposal. However, on his next leave, Joe and I decided to get married.

It was my happy duty to arrange for the Registrar to call at the little church of Saint Thomas More in our village of Eastcote, Middlesex, which had been recently consecrated and where my father had donated the new baptismal font.

The Registrar's office was a dismal place. I made inquiries and was asked to wait my turn. Just then a group of people arrived all a little the worse for drink. The Registrar entered, then a couple stood up. Someone threw a ring on the table and papers were signed. It was then I realised I was witnessing a civil wedding ceremony.

I was so struck by the sad features of the bride and the alcoholic giggling of the men that I nearly forgot the reason for my presence, until one of the inebriated males asked me if I had come to get married. However, when the tearful women and the tipsy men had departed, the

Registrar apologised for the mistake and I duly made arrangements for the wedding, appointed to take place on 13th January 1940, a little under four months from the day war was declared.

The white wedding took place at the Roman Catholic Church of Saint Thomas More at two o'clock in the afternoon. We exchanged vows and became man and wife to the sound of German bombers as they flew high above the church that sunny afternoon.

As we walked down the aisle after the ceremony, I caught the eye of a frail little woman dressed in black, wearing a stiff bowler-type hat, for which she was well known in the upper strata of London society. It was Lady Cadogan, mother of the British War Minister. She was now domiciled in a house near to my parents'; she had heard about the wedding from my father and had come to wish us well.

Our new home — a flat near Baker Street, London — was a very humble affair. I had gathered a few articles of furniture, but because the agent let us down at the last minute we had to make do without a kitchen, so that all cooking had to be done on a gas ring.

There was no honeymoon as leave passes were short, so we returned to the flat after the reception at my parents' home.

Our first meal consisted of lamb stew, which we left to simmer on the gas ring while we attended Sunday Mass at the magnificent old church of Saint James, Spanish Place. Ironically, the Gospel that Sunday was about the wedding feast of Cana, at Galilee. I must confess that my mind was on our feast and whether it had all boiled over!

24

Having little money for furniture, I covered orange boxes with brightly coloured cretonne to use as small cupboards and made bright cushions for the chairs. For warmth we had an electric fire and our only luxury was a radio set, television not yet being commonplace.

The view from the window was mainly of chimney pots, of which I counted 50.

There were visits to nearby Regent's Park and the London Zoo, but one week's leave wert all too quickly and there were many sad partings and happy reunions, matching the number of leave passes my husband could obtain.

I had my job to keep me busy at a wholesale clothes manufacturers, as the large fashion houses had begun to close their doors. The large buildings of London were now austere, with outer walls reinforced with piles of sandbags and the windows criss-crossed with strips of brown adhesive paper to prevent glass shattering should bombs explode nearby.

At night the streets were without lights and car lights were shaded to give only a glimmer. The only bright places were the Underground (tube) railway stations where bunk-beds had been installed and people of all ages and creeds prepared to bed down for the night. Children slept as passengers alighted from the trains and older people regaled themselves with snacks and hot drinks.

I had blacked-out my flat windows with thick material and the bathroom window was covered with brown paper — an unsatisfactory arrangement, as I was later to learn.

I was awoken one night by a loud banging on the door. "Who is it?" I called.

"The Police," came the reply.

I opened the door in my dressing gown. A uniformed policeman stood there. He said, "I will have to issue you with a summons to appear at Bow Street Magistrates' Court. You are charged with showing a light, thereby helping the enemy and ignoring blackout regulations."

I then remembered the bathroom window; the brown paper was inadequate.

A few weeks later the summons duly arrived. I had to take a day off work, find my way to Bow Street and wait my turn while some unpleasant fellows were shouting abuse at one another in the dock.

The time came for those accused of showing lights. My heart sank as the magistrate handed out fines of 50 and 60 pounds.

It was my turn and I nervously took my place beside the dock. The magistrate called my name — Mary Winifred Burke — and read out the details of my offence. "The fine will be ten pounds," he said.

Remembering my microscopic bank balance and my Army allowance of two pounds a week, I piped up, "I am sorry, Your Worship, I can't afford that. I am a soldier's wife." To my astonishment the reply came back instantly.

"Very well then," said His Worship, "three pounds, with time to pay."

Everyone in the court stared in amazement as I made my way out of the building, still quite astonished at being let off so lightly.

CHAPTER
FIVE

The Realities of War

My husband's leave passes became less frequent as the war dragged on. The news of ship sinkings filled the newspapers. The wail of the air raid sirens became regular and more frequent.

School children had been sent off to the country and the carrying of gas masks became compulsory. At about 9.30 every evening, the air raid sirens would wail with monotonous regularity, and then would come the deep throbbing sound of the German bombers, easily distinguishable from the British fighter planes.

We needed a new flat and found one on the ground floor of a large old-style house in Swiss Cottage, at the northern end of Regent's Park.

There was a basement where the owners — an old couple — lived, and two flats above ours. At the rear, there was a small garden, a large elm tree, and an air raid shelter.

Yes! We could have the flat, on condition there were no babies or animals. I smiled at this and noticed the family photographs on the antique mahogany sideboard placed in the lounge of their basement flat.

Once again my weekends were fully occupied turning the new flat into a home. The front room was palatial, with large bay windows and strong shutters on either side. The kitchen was smaller, with floor to ceiling windows overlooking a well cut lawn.

By this time the German Air Force — or Luftwaffe — were ready to unload their cargoes of bombs on London.

Life went on as usual during the day except for an occasional interruption for a visit to an air raid shelter, of which London was well provided. As soon as the siren sounded, usually at 9.30 p.m., we would take our sandwiches and thermos flasks filled with tea or coffee and retire to the garden shelter until the "All Clear" sounded, sometimes one hour or two later.

Sometimes our sleep would be interrupted in the early hours of the morning and we would drag our weary bodies wrapped in blankets back to the shelter. Sometimes we would hear the sound of an explosion and feel the earth tremble as a bomb exploded nearby, or see the glare of brilliant flares as they were dropped in clusters to light up the target for high explosive bombs.

The air raid wardens would be out on the streets, blowing their whistles and summoning fire brigades as fires blazed from bombed buildings. Ambulances were heard racing to stricken houses to rescue those buried beneath the rubble.

The Army bomb disposal units were in force to dig out bombs that had failed to explode. They were brave men and their task was hazardous in the extreme.

Our shelter became a little stuffy at times, for the only ventilation was the narrow entrance through which we had to crawl. The occupants included a German Jewish couple, recently escaped from Germany, a single lady and her boyfriend, small dog, myself and husband, when on leave. The owners preferred to stay in the basement.

It was a good time to finish my knitting, which helped to steady the nerves until the sirens sounded the "All Clear".

In spite of this, Joe and I were delighted to find that I was expecting our first child. Arrangements were made for me to attend the Middlesex Hospital in London, so I booked a bed for the middle of November 1940.

Apart from physical changes and the realisation that to attain a healthy babe a mental state of calm must be achieved life proceeded much as usual and I kept my job in the wholesale dress business.

The building in which I worked was well reinforced with sandbags. First aid lectures were given, but I soon found out that I was not cut out to be a nurse when the doctor, a well known heart specialist, brought with him a pickled heart with which to explain the circulatory system. The heart was passed for inspection from one student to another so quickly that someone remarked, "It's too hot to handle." The doctor apologised for its squashed appearance, saying he had been sitting on it in the car.

I attended the hospital at the given time of 9.30 a.m. once a month. It became horrifying to see the stretchers carried in, bearing the bodies of those killed and injured in the previous night's bombing. I would have to sit and wait my turn with all the other pregnant women from all parts of London. Some of their stories of narrow escapes and lost relatives were terrifying.

The newspapers were full of the good news and the sad news, the bravery of the airmen, known as "the first of the few" in the Battle of Britain, and the disaster of Dunkirk, when every available craft from the smallest rowing boat to a Thames barge was sent out to collect men who had had to retreat to the beaches of Dunkirk and were stranded on the French coast.

As if Germany was exhausted by the retaliation of our bombers and fighters, there seemed a short lull in the enemy assault on London.

The Underground railways had provided excellent shelter for thousands of people. Every evening there would be a long queue outside the Swiss Cottage tube station from 5 o'clock onwards. At 8 p.m. they were allowed to enter, old people, young people, and babes in arms. On more than one occasion a baby would be born unexpectedly on the platform. I remember an incident where women provided privacy for a young mother about to give birth by taking off their coats and standing in a circle, holding their coats up until first aid attendants could be summoned.

Quite often there was community singing led by some star of vaudeville, until the last train rattled out and sleep took over.

One night, an Underground station received a direct hit. There were bodies scattered everywhere and some heartrending work for the magnificent air raid wardens and Red Cross personnel.

My husband's next leave occurred in September 1940. It happened to be my birthday and we needed something to cheer us up. We started off by walking to Regent's

Park, then through Queen Mary's rose garden; we lingered over the bridge to watch the antics of the ducks on the quiet lake and the swans gliding lazily by when, looking up to the cloudless sky, we could hear the drone of German bombers. At that moment the sirens wailed and we took cover in the shelter provided on the perimeter of the park. The anti-aircraft guns were soon in action, the planes turned to a northerly direction and the All Clear sounded soon after.

We had some leave money to spend and, as it was my birthday, we decided to have a meal and go to a show, so we walked down Baker Street to Marble Arch.

The streets were full of khaki-clothed men and women, on leave or in transit; the WRENS, the ATS and the WRAF. Some had bandaged limbs, some were without limbs. Dunkirk had taken a heavy toll.

We arrived at the Princes Theatre in the West End of London and bought two tickets for a variety show called "Shepherd's Pie", produced by Firth Shephard. It was a gay, light-hearted show which we thoroughly enjoyed.

At 9.30 the air raid siren sounded; an announcement followed that "the show would go on". We were advised that it would be unwise to leave the building until the "All Clear" had sounded. The show proceeded to the tune of loud thuds and the crackle of the anti-aircraft guns, or "ack ack" as they were commonly known. The actors finished the show and took their last bow to heavy applause.

People chatted until tired. One young man grabbed the microphone and started to sing until someone switched him off.

I remember seeing a velvet couch in the foyer, so we walked over to it and I laid my pregnant body down to sleep, with Joe seated beside me.

We were there about 15 minutes when a very frightened air raid warden, wearing a tin hat and siren suit, almost tumbled down a narrow stairway shouting, "Everyone in the dugout on the floor." Hastily we retreated to the dugout, which happened to be the bar, heavily reinforced with sandbags.

We learned that incendiary bombs had fallen on the roof. Incendiaries usually meant that high explosives were next. We were lying like sardines, together with the cast of the show and hundreds of other people, until it became hot and stuffy. The only alternative was to lie under the seats in the theatre and try to snatch some sleep until the All Clear sounded at 6 a.m., meaning we could all return to our homes.

On entering the street we could see that the sky was crimson. At first we thought it was a brilliant sunrise, until we were told that the dock areas had been devastated. Warehouses and other buildings were lying in heaps of rubble.

This had been one of the biggest raids of the war. We managed to get a taxi, although many roads were impassable owing to unexploded bombs. It was Sunday morning, so we attended Mass and then went home to bed.

CHAPTER
SIX

Adjusting to War

The elderly couple who owned the house in which we lived were kindly people, and although I told them I was expecting our baby in November 1940, they had not asked us to leave, but regaled my appetite with an occasional steak and kidney pie or a home baked cake.

We kept the flat clean and were quiet tenants. The only intrusion was the distant rumblings of the bombing of London.

As the evenings grew colder we found it difficult to leave our warm beds. I suggested to the other tenants and my husband, when home on leave, that it would be just as safe if we all slept in our large living room. We had an extra divan wide enough for Walter and Gerda — the Jewish couple who lived in the first floor flat — and a single chair bed for the lady on the second floor. We slept in our double bed behind a screen in a corner of the room. The owners preferred to stay in the basement flat.

The tenants all agreed to this and bedded down each night as if in a commune. We hoped that the strong ceiling would give us protection.

One night there was a terrific crash nearby. I remember the others trying to stop me going to the front door. Terrified people were running down the street in their night clothes.

Walter and Gerda were hoping to go to America, where they had friends. They owned a magnificent grand piano, which they offered to sell to me for 11 pounds.

I have always regretted having to refuse that offer. Gerda would play "Ave Maria" for me while Walter sang in a deep baritone voice. I often wonder whether they made it to America.

Instructions arrived from the Middlesex Hospital for the evacuation of all expectant mothers in London to the country at a given date. I wrote and told Joe and packed my bags with enough clothing for a few months, not forgetting clothes for the baby.

The problem was getting to the coach with two heavy bags, but Walter came to my aid and carried them to the appointed bus station. About 30 expectant mothers piled into the coach, all ready for the mystery tour. We were not told of our destination. We soon left the sandbagged buildings, passed through the northern suburbs of London into the green belt areas, through winding country roads and then on to the highways.

I looked around at my fellow travellers. Some were Cockneys cracking jokes with a loud laugh, on perhaps their first ever country holiday. Some were wives of soldiers, sailors or airmen.

One lady was rather fond of the gin bottle, another had her coat fastened by a safety pin. She was having her seventh child. All her other children, she told us, had gone to billets in the country with their schools.

The autumn countryside seemed peaceful enough, with the leaves tinged in gold in the misty sunlight. Soon we were climbing the hill to Stamford, a solidly built city surmounted by an ancient cathedral.

All street names had been obliterated for security reasons and after several hours in the coach we were deposited at a building known as the Old Infirmary, which had been turned into an emergency hospital.

We were greeted with cups of tea by ladies wearing the dark green uniform of the Women's Voluntary Service. We were to be billeted with local residents. A law had been passed requiring residents to take at least two evacuees.

While allocations were proceeding, we were told we would have time to wash. I still remember the lady with the safety pins saying, "Wash? What do we want to wash for?"

When my name was called I was introduced to a homely lady and invited to get into the car waiting outside. She drove me back to a solidly built house just near the cathedral, I could tell from the brass plate beside the door that I was entering into the home of a doctor and his wife.

I was shown into an oak-panelled room with a comfortable bed and carpeted floor.

My new friend's baby was asleep in his cot, and her husband returned later after a busy day at the clinic.

I unpacked my bags and after a delicious meal was glad to have a good night's sleep.

We were now well into October and I kept myself busy by helping in the house and accompanying my new friend on walks through the fields with her young son in the pram.

Stamford in Lincolnshire, with its cobbled streets and quaint shops, was a delight I had not anticipated. There was plenty of knitting to do and the joy of watching the doctor's baby son having his bath.

My husband was now stationed at a distant training camp on the other side of England.

On attending the ante-natal clinic it was found that I might have a "breech" baby. I was a little concerned. My newly found friends had prepared me for the first signs of the expected birth, and I was to awaken them immediately the labour pains began.

One night, I woke suddenly, not with labour pains but in fright as I heard some scratching underneath the panelling. A mouse was trying to make a breakthrough and I am terrified of these verminous creatures. I put the light on and threw my shoe at the panelled wall. Just then an air raid siren began to wail and I could hear the throbbing sound of German bombers. Then the labour pains began and I had to wake the sleeping doctor and his wife, who transported me in her car to the emergency hospital, three miles away.

There were dull thuds of distant explosions and the ack-ack crackled angrily. It was a clear November night as the searchlights scanned the chill starlit sky.

The hospital was quite inadequate for the large numbers of women who were about to give birth that night. I was taken to the labour room and left alone for about four hours and told to press a switch when the pains became unbearable. I was cold and could hear the screams of the other women, but I was determined to remain as calm as possible, to be aware of the miracle of birth which was about to take place.

The doctor examined me and assured me the head would appear first, and it would not be a breech baby after all.

I mentally said a few prayers until pain took over, and I found myself surrounded by midwives. A voice kept saying, "push, push." I grabbed somebody's arm and I fear I dug my nails in deep. My head was hot with sweat while I felt my teeth physically chatter with cold.

"Come on — be a good girl," the voice urged, and then someone slapped an oxygen mask on my mouth. I breathed deeply, gulping the air greedily, then with one final exhausted effort I heard the high-pitched cry of my baby.

Relieved that the pain was over, I just wanted to fall asleep, but was aroused by a voice speaking sharply: "You have a little girl — don't you want to see her? I've no patience with mothers who don't want their children," the voice continued.

I was given a cup of tea and the little red bundle was placed beside me. I examined the small round head and perfect features of my daughter, the bright red hair and blue eyes. She was snug and warm, but I was still shivering and had to be given extra blankets and hot water bottles.

The mother in the opposite bed to mine just stared into space and did not speak. I was told that her husband had just been killed in action. She had a baby son.

As I gazed at the women sitting up in bed in their freshly laundered nightgowns, newly washed faces gleaming in the sunny ward and bathed in the joy of motherhood, it occurred to me that here I was in the presence of angels.

The miracle of birth concluded, the months of waiting and the double hazard of war had left an almost mystical glow on each countenance that was very near to Heaven.

Next day, after the doctor's visit, there was some talk of my temperature being alarmingly high. I would have to be moved into an isolated room. It was some kind of fever, but the doctors in those days never discussed reasons for treatment with the patient. Baby was taking her milk well but cuts appeared on my nipples. I desperately wanted to breast feed, so that balsam, methylated spirits and all kinds of cures were used to heal the cuts. Finally, a shield was needed.

Breast feeding became painful, but my determination left me steadfast. One sister, a relic from a past era of nursing, would answer my pleas for more sanitary protection. "You can't have another towel as every one means a dead sailor," she would reply, meaning that they had to be imported from America and many ships had recently been sunk. Consequently my fever had increased; there was infection.

Letters came from my husband, who was somewhere in England on an intensive training course. He was very happy about the baby but there was a war on and he could not get leave for at least four weeks. My parents did manage to come and visit me, but had to return the same day to be home before the siren sounded at night.

On the third day after the birth, a sister told me to prepare for a ride in an ambulance to a sanatorium; it was useless to ask why, although it was obvious the nurses were rushed off their feet and too busy to discuss anything.

As long as the baby came too and I was under hospital care, at least it was better than staring at four walls. A nice little trip in the ambulance was a welcome break.

The countryside was now in late autumn, and the leaves were lying lifeless on the chilled earth. The baby had not cried once and seemed to enjoy the closeness and vibration of the vehicle. It was intriguing to watch the concerned faces of the passers-by. I could see them through the darkened windows, but they couldn't see me.

At last we arrived at two large gates, drove up a long winding path and stopped at the main hall of what was described on a nearby sign as Leicester Sanatorium.

We were taken on a stretcher bed to a long row of one storey buildings and placed in a small room, well heated but with a double door opening on to a grassy lawn. My baby, whom I had named Josephine Mary, was snatched away from me and taken to the nursery. By that time I was hungry. Nurses appeared regularly but never stopped long enough to answer questions.

I was handed a warm drink and waited patiently for my meal to arrive. I had fed the baby but had not eaten since breakfast.

Evening came and at long last the food tray appeared. On my plate was a portion of what looked like washed white blanket, peas and potatoes in their skins. I was told that this was tripe, regarded as a delicacy in Leicester. I couldn't eat it, so made do with the rice pudding to follow. No use complaining; the stock phrase was, "Don't you know, there's a war on?"

My milk supply, of course, temporarily disappeared, and I was told that baby was given a supplementary bottle of milk in the nursery.

I fell into an exhausted sleep but was awoken by a sister shining a torch in my face.

"Are you awake?" she enquired.

"Yes," I replied, "I am now."

"Take this sleeping tablet." She pushed a glass of water in front of me and waited until I had swallowed the pill.

I was awakened at 5 a.m., given a cup of tea and a bowl of warm water with which to wash my face and hands. The next two hours I spent longing for some breakfast. When it arrived, it was lumpy porridge, a cup of tea and two thick slices of bread and margarine.

After breakfast I was placed on a stretcher and taken to the operating theatre for a thorough examination. I was strung up like a chicken with a thick woollen sock on each foot.

The doctor was of dark appearance, young, cheerful, but very ugly. He resembled a picture I had seen of Dracula; not that I was frightened of him, but I wondered why he had not discussed with me the reason for this sudden drastic checkup.

I was then catheterised, or subject to having an instrument inserted to draw off the urine. After the examination was completed and my inquiry as to the result received a blank expression from Doctor Dracula, I was duly despatched to my room.

The next day I wrote letters and read a little while my door was left wide open to the chill Leicestershire air.

The following night I was kept awake by Doctor Dracula's whistling and singing in a deep baritone voice as he hurried up the corridor at regular intervals.

A week had gone by and I was feeling stronger. Even the Luftwaffe had left us alone until one fearful night, the night of the bombing and devastation of nearby Coventry, cases began to arrive thick and fast. The doctor was worked off his feet while ambulances arrived every few minutes with mothers about to give birth and, sadly, those mothers whose babies were stillborn.

Each day I was allowed to get up for short periods, but it was decided that the journey home would be too exhausting, so arrangements were made for me to go and stay in Stamford with the kindly doctor and his wife until I had gathered strength.

There was no frilly cot in which to place the babe, so we simply pulled out the wardrobe drawer, placed a pillow inside it and laid down a rubber sheet, and lo and behold — there was our bassinet!

I was allowed to use the outside laundry, but there was only cold water, and washing nappies in cold water seemed like very hard work.

One foggy morning soon after my arrival, when I had started to hang nappies on the clothes line in the garden, the deafening noise of a plane swooping low frightened me. It swooped over the rooftops, at the same time splattering the roofs with machine gun fire. It certainly caught the air raid warden napping that time. I learned that the roof on the inn at the corner of the square received the full brunt of the attack.

CHAPTER
SEVEN

On the Move Again

The voice of Winston Churchill was frequently heard over the radio, at this time exhorting the British people to greater war efforts. We gained strength from his encouraging words and heeded his warnings that German paratroops could be parachuted into any country area by day or night. In that event the church bells would ring to warn the Home Guard and villagers.

Meanwhile, letters arrived from my husband with place names deleted and for security reasons were heavily censored. My replies were sent to a Central Army Post Office and then despatched to him.

A letter came from my parents inviting me to stay with them at my former home in Eastcote. I accepted their offer and my father travelled by train to Stamford to collect myself and baby Josephine. After thanking the kindly doctor and his wife, we were soon on the train to London, where we had to change on to the Underground railway.

Unfortunately, my father had to attend a meeting in town, so I continued on my own, carrying my pink bundle and dealing with a large case as well as I could.

By the time we arrived at Wembley station, the snow was falling fast, and to my surprise the guard called out,

"All Change," causing a short delay until the Eastcote train arrived.

At last we drew into our destination. I gathered up my precious cargo and struggled up the slope to the exit, where I hoped to get a taxi. There was a mile to go, no bus service, and not a taxi in sight. A car came over the bridge. I hailed the car. It was driven by a man in his thirties. I explained my predicament. "I'm a doctor — I'll take you to your door," he said. I thanked him warmly and alighted with bundle and baggage intact.

I knocked on the door but there was no answer, so I sought refuge with our neighbours next door. My poor mother had gone to the next station, where there was a bus service which stopped at the corner of our road. It all ended happily, however, when she returned and extracted a warm meal from the oven which she had prepared before she left home.

The next day, arrangements were made for the baptism in the church where I had been married earlier that year, and we would use my father's presentation font.

Joe was granted a week's leave and once again there was great happiness as the two families came together for the baptism of our first child.

There was, however, another move in the offing. We had seen a two-bedroomed house, newly built and at a low rental on the outskirts of Ruislip — the next railway station after Eastcote. It was only three miles from Mum and Dad, and had a small garden.

I wasted no time in contacting a removal firm and we were soon installed.

My aunt, a nun at a convent in nearby Hertfordshire, on hearing of our move, wrote asking if we could accommodate General de Gaulle's secretary. It appeared that the General was living nearby, attending Mass at the convent, and was unable to find accommodation for the lady. Unfortunately, I had to refuse as there were only two bedrooms and very little furniture.

Six weeks later my husband was granted another week's leave, in which he decided we should visit his parents who lived in Barnes, Surrey. They told us that they had seen a charming flat only a few doors from their large double-fronted two-storey house which faced a lake, complete with picturesque trees and shrubs and swans nesting on a central island in the lake. The house boasted a front balcony and we could have the first and second floors.

The offer seemed tempting as the rent was low and, of course, they would see more of their soldier son.

Once again the removal men were called in and bundled our scant amount of furniture to the new address in Barnes, not far from the delightful parkland known as Barnes Common.

Joe's mother gave us an old Rose Wilton carpet for the large sitting room. It was not new but in good condition. After a few weeks of exploring the delights of Barnes Common and the quaint High Street, or taking a bus to the City of London, my sister came to visit. She admired the flat and, seeing the possibilities as a mecca for her newly acquired friends, she asked if she could use our large sitting room for the purpose of entertaining them for a special occasion.

Since the Germans had given us some respite from the bombing, possibly due to the presence of barrage balloons which now made it impossible for planes to fly over the centre of the City, I agreed.

Everything was left ready for the party, dishes of food were prepared and left ready the night before.

Before retiring for the night I had placed a few nappies to air around the open fire. We slept peacefully for some time until I was awakened to the sound of someone shouting, "Fire — Fire!"

I grabbed the baby, said to my husband, "The house is on fire," roused my sister, and quickly descended the stairs. I passed the kitchen door; smoke was billowing out.

I placed the baby on a divan on the ground floor and went to help the people who were carrying buckets of water upstairs. The owner of the flat, who lived an the ground floor, was using a stirrup pump on the smouldering floor boards, which proved very effective. A stirrup pump was the most efficient way of dealing with incendiaries.

All the paintwork had blistered. The radio set had fallen apart, the curtains burnt to ribbons. The heat from the fire had burst the water pipe under the sink, and if it wasn't for the sound of water flowing down into the flat below, we would all have been burned alive.

After the fire was put out, my husband appeared in the doorway in his dressing gown. He had gone back to sleep after the initial call, unable to find his dressing gown.

There was no time to notify the guests and we did manage to cook up a few goodies for a short party.

Next day we assessed the damage and the landlord consulted the insurance company. Apart from the shocking inconvenience, he was adequately reimbursed and, being a builder of some repute, all was not lost.

After returning to barracks, my husband found that he had been transferred to Wiltshire, and applied for us to be billeted near his Army camp. The War Office by this time had relaxed its censorship of place names, and I was faced with yet another move, at the same time keeping the flat while we took up a new life in a little village called Codford, with only a main street nestling in the heart of the English countryside.

The cottage where we stayed was small and boasted a thatched roof. There was a bedroom with a hand basin and shower and toilet in the yard. The roof and walls were supported by oak beams. Here and there was a piece of wood jutting from the wall beam, and known as a wig post, a relic from the old days.

There was a lodger, an old man who drove a steamroller and one day proudly showed me his medals. Unfortunately, closer inspection revealed the name inscribed on the rim of the medals was not his name at all.

Soon the cottage accommodation became a little cramped, with the baby as well, so we started to search for something a little bigger.

We only had to visit the village grocer for all the local news, where I was told that a lady living on her own had a larger cottage where the upstairs rooms were vacant. There was a garden with a real wishing well containing pure fresh spring water, complete with wooden bucket which had to be lowered by a handle. The living room had a log fire and beside it an old iron oven, but in the small back room was an oil cooking stove complete with well behaved oven, except for the time when I left the oil burners too high, burned the potatoes and blackened the ceiling.

Miss Oxford, as she was known, was a pleasant spinster lady who occupied the ground floor of the picturesque cottage.

The bathroom with toilet was a recent addition and, although not decorated, was spotlessly clean. The only disadvantage was having to walk through the landlady's living room before we could ascend the squeaky stairs to our apartment, but Miss Oxford, a charming person, often acted as babysitter whenever there was a dance at the Sergeants'' Mess in my husband's camp.

Our peace in Wiltshire was only disturbed by an occasional tank trundling past the cottage. I would be lying in bed in the early morning when suddenly a man's head would be peering through the window. I had forgotten that the tanks were as high as a house, and when the soldiers had to stop suddenly outside there would be loud laughter as I dived under the sheets.

The Army allowance was barely enough to pay for food and clothing, so I decided to try obtaining a job in Salisbury, our nearest town. I sought out the nearest crèche for young Josephine and was lucky to find a job in one of the biggest stores, named Blooms. Josephine was now a toddler and took well to the spacious nursery, with trained staff and visiting doctor. The children had plenty of room to play in the open air, and when sleepy could lie down after lunch on one of the many little canvas beds.

The job was easy and quite well paid, comprising of fittings and dress alterations attached to the dress salon.

All went well for a few months and I was able to save a little money, until Joe arrived home saying that his training in this camp was now finished and that it was back to our London flat once again.

CHAPTER
EIGHT

From Pillar to Post

After the fire incident, we were asked to find alternative accommodation, but as luck would have it I found the very thing in a quiet street named Elm Grove Road, close to transport and Bames Common.

The flat was on the ground floor and this time I had three rooms, bathroom and toilet. I moved in with Josephine and Joe came home occasionally on leave.

Josephine was now a darling and intelligent little girl with red bronze hair. We were great companions, but she needed the company of other children and having found a job in the West End of London at my old fashion house of Jacqmar, I decided to get up at 6 a.m. and take her to the local day nursery, where she would have adequate attention.

It was quite a struggle getting up on dark winter mornings, getting her washed and dressed.

The bus stopped outside the nursery, and I was soon scurrying off to earn a little money to supplement the meagre Army Wives Allowance of just over two pounds a week. At night I would rush back, bring her home, cook a meal, play with her, and then set about cleaning up the flat.

One morning I dressed her and noticed that she was limping. I insisted that the doctor examine her when he called. I worried quite a bit at work and rushed back to the nursery at five o'clock to find all the nurses laughing and giggling.

"What was the trouble?" I inquired with an alarmed expression.

"You put two legs in one hole of her panties," they replied.

We were now two years into the war and I had once again become pregnant, much to my delight because I was desperately hoping for a son. I had not been blessed with brothers so that I looked forward to a brother for Josephine and kept working at Jacqmar's until quite near the expected date of birth.

The nearest maternity hospital in the Surrey area was at Kingston-upon-Thames, where I had made a prior booking. This time my husband was granted compassionate leave and was allowed to visit me after our new baby son was born.

With regular visits from my husband and friends, I did not have to suffer the isolation of my first confinement. Joe was equally delighted at the good news and treated the children with tender loving care.

We spent many happy days in Bames until a letter from Joe arrived. I had become accustomed to moving, so that it was no great hardship when I learned that he was now stationed in Yorkshire.

I was to bring the children to the village of Middleham in the North Riding, where he had procured a comfortable billet for us.

The next days were spent gathering up articles of clothing, packing a large case and preparing to go to the north of England. We arranged to keep the flat and, as the Government paid a large percentage of our fare and billet money, we could just afford it.

The trains were mostly full of servicemen. Everyone was willing to help on noticing me struggle with two children, luggage and a pram. There was the problem of breast feeding Kevin, so I entered a carriage which contained mostly women and one man. Seeing that I was discreetly breast feeding the child, he thoughtfully stepped into the corridor.

We arrived at Northallerton Junction, where we had to change to a branch line for Middleham. Joe was already waiting with a large Army vehicle. After warm greetings we bumped along the winding lane that skirted the lonely moors, until we came to an old world village. We stopped at a solidly built granite house. I was told that many years ago it had served as the Old Wine House attached to Middleham Castle, the ruins of which could be seen in the background. Historians had revealed that Mary, Queen of Scots, had once taken refuge within those stalwart walls.

We were greeted at the front door by a buxom lady wearing a spotless white overall and learned that her name was Mrs Weatherill. She had a kind but firm expression, and a healthy countenance.

The aroma of freshly baked bread assailed our nostrils, coming from the large kitchen range at the far end of the living room. Everything was spick and span and the table was laid for high tea. She invited us to take our place. The table was spread with a white linen cloth and the food was of the highest quality.

Next day I helped in the house where possible while Kevin slept in his pram outside the back door. Josephine followed me about or played with her toys.

Mr Weatherill was a stockily built man with a friendly Yorkshire accent; a little too friendly when he caught me hanging out the washing. He would playfully tickle me under the arms. He soon stopped when I threatened to tell his wife.

One night, hearing footsteps outside the window, I pulled the curtain aside, only to see an armed Grenadier Guardsman patrolling up and down at the rear of the house, but at the same time singing the song "Moonlight Becomes You", possibly thinking of his girl friend and to break the monotony of the night patrol.

I then imagined a group of German parachutists landing to the refrain of "Lili Marlene". How much better than fighting. C'est la guerre!

Although the war was taking all kinds of new turns, it was comparatively quiet in Middleham except for the clatter of the King's horses as they cantered through the village with their trainers for a gallop on the moors, the stable being owned by Matt Peacock, King George the Sixth's trainer. They were also evacuated to Middleham.

Matt Peacock's sister was a friend of the Weatherills and would call daily with a plate of semolina and cheese sandwiches for the troops. I often wondered if they enjoyed the mixture.

Sunday lunch was a great event. After returning from Mass at the nearest church, we would be greeted by the aroma of roast beef, and of course the Yorkshire pudding, which was superb, with apple pie waiting to be served afterwards.

The children loved to go for a walk up the hill and onto the moors; vast acres of infertile, undulating hills, some yellow with buttercups, some white with daisies or covered with bluebells, making a kind of patchwork quilt. We had to pass the sentry box at the summit of the hill and give my name to the sentry, although I hardly looked like a spy with one baby in the pram and one child walking beside me. But if a mist descended, one could possibly lose one's sense of direction. On the way back we would pass through the stable of Matt Peacock, who always had a smile and a joke for the children, and a coin for their hands.

One night I offered to make the cocoa before retiring. Everyone complained of the terrible taste, making the most excruciating faces. I think they all suspected I was trying to poison them with arsenic, until I glanced inside the large copper kettle and found the rubber tube extension to the cold tap had fallen off and was floating inside, giving added body to the boiled cocoa water.

Once, when walking in the field behind the castle, I saw an old lady running towards the gate. I opened the gate for her and a deep manly voice said, "Thank you." It was a jockey, heavily rugged up, trying to lose a few pounds before the weigh-in.

Summer turned to autumn and once again the Grenadier Guards were on the move back to London. It was time to say goodbye to the wonderful country people of Yorkshire.

The war was nearly into its third year. Many Grenadiers of the Third Battalion had lost their lives at Dunkirk. My husband was now to be transferred to the newly formed Fourth Battalion, which was stationed at Victoria Barracks, Windsor. There were whispers of an expected German invasion of England, when Hitler then did an extraordinary thing, sending his troops towards Russia, even surprising his own generals.

We returned to our flat in Bames and soon after Joe was given a short spell of leave and prepared me for the news that we had been expecting since war broke out. He was to be sent abroad and was not allowed to divulge the destination. Because of the frequent sinking of troopships, it was dangerous to even talk in one's sleep.

The day came for him to leave. There was no room for tears; we had become used to saying hello and goodbye. The only request he had made was for a photograph of the three of us, to carry in his breast pocket.

The photograph was produced. I was wearing a dark red velvet blouse I had made, and held Kevin on my knee, with Josephine leaning against me with her little arm around my neck. And so . . . he left.

For the next few days there was an empty feeling, but with prayer and a love of life, there was plenty to do.

I still had my loving parents, and there was Joe's mother who, in spite of the fact she had five sons to worry about, was bearing her burden very well.

After a month a letter arrived from Joe, heavily censored with addresses obliterated, so that I had no clue as to his whereabouts. My replies were sent first to an Army Post Office and then redirected.

Christmas came and we made it as happy for the children as possible. There was an occasional pantomime or a party with friends. The flat was clean and comfortable, there were curtains to make, also covers for chairs. The people upstairs seemed pleasant enough, although on occasions they could be heard arguing loudly. The wife was in her thirties and had a young son aged 12. The husband appeared to be about 60, of moderate height, and spoke with an Irish accent.

One morning I slipped on my recently made quilted satin dressing gown, turned on the cold tap to fill the kettle for a cup of tea, when the top of the tap flew off. A fountain of water shot up to the ceiling and began to drench me and fill the kitchen. I yelled, "Help!" The couple soon appeared in the doorway but all they could do was laugh. Not being in a humorous mood, I groped around for the main tap, although I still can't remember how I stopped the flood.

As time went on, the arguments from upstairs seemed to get worse, until one day a vacuum cleaner took wing and came flying down the stairs. A few days later a broom had a similar fate. Finally, the lady told me she was taking her son away, leaving the old man to his drinking problem.

I was exceedingly alarmed at being alone in the house with a drunken man and the added danger of flying missiles. The flats were not self-contained and the stairs led into the hallway, my bedroom being close to the front door. There was a cot on one side of the room, my bed, and a single bed for Josephine.

It was very late one night when I heard noises at the front door and heard a man shouting and swearing, falling about and fumbling for his key. I was very frightened. I grabbed my dressing gown and ran out of the back door shouting for help, but no answer came. I ran around the back passageway into the road and knocked on the door of a friend who lived opposite, asking if I could use the phone. I called the police.

After a few minutes a police car arrived. I showed them the doorway. Someone had taken the man's key and pushed him inside, where he lay in a heap just outside my bedroom door, so that I could neither get in nor out. Luckily, the children slept soundly throughout the drama.

The police finally shifted the body up the stairs and said that, as he was in the house, there wasn't much they could do. However, not being accustomed to dealing with elderly drunks, my father being a strict teetotaller, and my mother occasionally indulging in a glass of wine — home-made, elderberry or parsnip — I was determined not to spend another night in that place.

The next day I packed up the bags and the children, and took the train to Eastcote where my parents, on hearing the story of the drunken tenant, welcomed me and the children.

It was peaceful, sitting in the garden of my old home once again and chatting to my mother as my father pottered around, tending the plants, but the peace was interrupted by the approach of a telegraph boy. I felt a chill go down my spine as I looked at the envelope. It was addressed to me, but I handed it to my father to open. "Come at once," it read, "bomb has landed near your flat in Elm Grove." It was from Joe's parents.

I returned at once. The road had been cordoned off and a policeman was on duty at the barrier. He questioned me and I told him that my home was at number sixty-eight. I was allowed to pass and hurried down the road, where there was a large crater.

Every window had been blown out of the house and the doors were hanging on by one hinge. I walked into the bedroom and was shocked to see the beds covered in splinters of broken glass, one inch thick.

I looked at the cot and the single bed. They also were smothered in slivers of glass from the windows and the wardrobe. We would have either been killed or severely injured. Dust was everywhere.

A high-explosive bomb had made a direct hit on a house a few doors down the road. I was told that many dead bodies had been carried away that night and many others were seriously injured.

I went to a phone and called a storage firm to arrange collection of what was left of the furniture and then returned to my parents and the children.

For the next few weeks my parents gave us shelter, but they were getting on in years, and to be landed with a daughter and two children was not easy for them.

Every day I would scan the newspapers for accommodation or cycle a few miles looking for rooms or a flat — without any luck. I was told that if someone died, there would be a long queue waiting outside the house inquiring when the room would be free.

After many long searches, I was looking through a Catholic newspaper and saw an advertisement: "Lady needs companion, child not objected to". Well, I had two, but I took a chance and answered it. She replied that she would call and see me, which she did.

She was a tall spinster lady who lived with her father near Redhill and required someone to do light housework, although she had a cleaning lady. It was a large house in its own grounds near a very pretty village. She had no objection to children, being "Brown Owl" in the Girl Guides, and quite used to them. I once again picked up my bundles and took a train to Redhill where she met me with the car.

The house was large and had a long garden with plenty of fresh vegetables and a gardener to keep it tidy. A heap of sand was brought in to make a sandpit for the children. There were delightful country walks surrounding the house.

From the bedroom window I could see and hear the never-ending stream of tanks, armoured cars, trucks and ambulances rambling down to the English coast for the final onslaught which was to put an end to the war in Europe.

The Americans had now joined forces with Britain, together with the Canadians, Australian and troops from other allied countries, all poised for the final attack on Europe.

My sister, Amy, had met a Canadian officer, and had sailed to Canada to get married, in spite of the dangers of ships being sunk. After their honeymoon at Niagara Falls, her husband had been sent back to Britain and was stationed in Redhill. He would often arrive in a jeep with some of his tall Canadian pals for a cup of tea and a chat.

However, my sister, having joined the Canadian Red Cross, soon returned to England to spend a little time with her husband before he was posted to Europe.

The Germans had now begun to use a new weapon known a the V1 or Pilotless Flying Bomb. It was propelled like a rocket. When the fuel supply ran out it descended in silence, gathering speed so that it was hard to ascertain where it would land.

On one occasion, the gardener was busily digging when we heard the buzzing sound of on approaching rocket. It could be seen, travelling at high speed. Then silence. I gathered the children together and the gardener shouted, "Duck!" We lay prostrate on the ground. Suddenly the earth shook. There was a loud explosion. We recovered, still trembling. The gardener grabbed his bike and raced off to see if his home had been damaged. He returned shortly with the news that a row of cottages had been demolished, quite nearby.

The sirens still kept us awake at night and there were many trips to the safest part of the house, which was a cupboard under the stairs.

Someone would make tea and the children were given orange juice, which happened to be part of the Government's free supply to all children in wartime.

To the children, this became a new game. Even when the sirens had not sounded, they still became accustomed to waking in the night for their glass of orange juice.

Often our spinster friend would bring her Girl Guides home for their various activities, one of which was to learn how to bath a baby.

Seeing that I had the real thing, I was approached.

Imagine a bathroom full of giggling girls and one seven-month-old baby — delighted to have so much attention, and who still blushes when I remind him of his past history.

CHAPTER
NINE

A Home of Our Own

Many happy months were spent in that village near Redhill. The children were happy and healthy.

There was only one cloud on the horizon, and that revolved around Kevin, now able to stand up in his cot.

Whether it was the nightly jaunts caused by the air raids or teething problems which had affected his sleep, he seemed to have developed a feeling of insecurity and would give out the most piercing screams every night. The screams became so unbearable that it was beginning to upset the sleep of the whole household, and I was becoming rather unpopular. Babies were supposed to be dear little things who slept normally all night through.

In the daytime he were a sweet passive child, admired for his beautifully shaped head and short, chestnut gold hair.

Finally, after a lot of frustration, I decided to take the children back to Eastcote where we would all feel more secure. Not forgetting the kindness of our friends at Redhill, we were soon back with my parents, who so often came to the rescue.

The war was now in its final stages. Europe was alive with advancing troops.

Letters from my husband had become fewer, until I received a typewritten "pep" letter from the War Office:

"We wish to inform you that your husband is safe after two years' service in North Africa. He is now fighting in Italy and has had a bath."

I read the last phrase over and over again and then I remembered the news reports and saw news pictures of soldiers fighting in a sea of mud. The men were literally eating and sleeping when they could; advancing in a rain-soaked country. There was no similarity to the sun-drenched Italy shown in the pre-war travel posters. My mind had not grasped the extent of the misery the men were enduring.

My husband had showered every day, his uniform spotless, buttons polished, shoes gleaming with a brilliant shine, and now here they were, crawling in mud, weighed down with a heavy back-pack — but at least he was still alive.

The year dragged on. There was little entertainment anywhere, only an occasional film.

We sang "The White Cliffs of Dover" to cheer ourselves up. The British Broadcasting Corporation provided plenty of good variety shows and the Entertainments National Service Association, or ENSA as it was known, presented lunchtime concerts in the munitions factories.

My efforts to find another flat were unending. I had heard of a flat in Chelsea, London, with a small back garden. The rent was thirty shillings a week, and more than I could afford on my small Army wives' allowance of two pounds a week.

My father was well into his seventies and I felt it was too much for him to be burdened with a young family. After the tension of four years of war, my nerves had become a little strained and I knew that I was becoming difficult to live with. We needed a home of our own in which I could prepare for my husband's return.

It was an autumn evening when I decided that my father should have the peace he richly deserved. The children were a little too noisy and, although he loved us all, I realised that it was difficult for him to cope in his advancing years.

The crisis came one evening when I realised that the situation was desperate and I had to think up a new idea for exploration.

When I was a young girl I had gone to the southeast coast for summer holidays. Many people had evacuated their homes there for the period of the war.

I wasted no time. Almost as the idea entered my head, I was off. My mother agreed to keep the children for a day or two until I had found a home.

It was seven o'clock in the evening when I reached Victoria Station and scanned the train timetable. There was a train in for Brighton. Should I take that one? I quite like Brighton. I had been to stay there many years ago with my grandmother. On the other hand there was a train due for Margate in half an hour. I decided to take the ticket for Margate.

Victoria Station looked chill and uninviting; the forces were prominent in their khaki, navy and blue uniforms, scurrying by on their wartime business. The train was crowded.

I took a corner seat and for some unknown reason I began to weep — just a few stifled tears. The soldiers were well behaved and spoke quietly to each other. Luckily the carriage was blacked out, and if they noticed me, they were tactfully polite.

All the time I was seated in that train I knew I was doing the right thing. It seemed that something was guiding me like a bird that flies, relying on its instinct to find — eventually — a resting place.

It was a slow train. The carriage began to empty until I was alone for the last two stations. It was 11 p.m. when the train arrived at Margate. The exit was deserted except for a few ancient taxis outside the entrance. I gained new life from the smell of the fresh sea air. I spoke to the first taxi driver on the rank.

"Can you take me to a clean, reasonable boarding house?" I asked.

"Hop in," he replied.

We sped quickly along the deserted promenade, with the wind whistling across the English Channel, over the sandy beach, climbed the short hill at the far side of the harbour and turned into a road leading from the chalk cliffs.

The taxi stopped outside a large, clean, double-fronted boarding house. I paid the driver, walked up the steps to the entrance hall, and was greeted by a homely lady who obviously had many years of experience in the boarding house business. She quietly ushered me to a room with bed and wash basin. It was clean, and without more ado

I undressed, laid my head on the pillow and was soon fast asleep.

Morning came; I felt the breeze from the sea. I felt renewed energy and was ready for a hearty breakfast of bacon and eggs. I took my place at the table in the dining room next to a tall, thin, elderly lady who was seated next to her friend.

We started up a conversation. I told her that I had come to Margate to look for a home for my children and husband on his return from the war.

She told me that she had two houses for sale in nearby Cliftonville. I told her that I could not possibly afford to buy a house.

"Well," said the lady, "just have a look and we'll see what we can do."

She wrote down the addresses of the houses, which were situated near a beautiful park. She then handed me the keys and told me where to contact her.

It was a sunny morning when I walked across the park. There were two roads leading from it and the house I was to look at was halfway down the second turning. They were terraced houses but in good condition, the windows criss-crossed with brown adhesive tape.

There was a bay window overlooking a small front garden. The front entrance led through to one large room divided into two by two well-constructed doors, so that it could serve as two separate rooms. The kitchen was at the far end of the hallway and also led into a scullery and a door into the back garden.

Upstairs, there were three bedrooms — a large bedroom in front with two long windows, a side bedroom, bathroom, toilet, and small rear bedroom.

Every room had a porcelain bell push which had connotations of bygone days when maids were plentiful and one had only to press a knob and some poor little underpaid skivvy would appear, trembling on the threshold.

I explored the garden. It was overgrown with weeds. On further scrutiny I saw some morello cherry trees, often used in the making of cherry brandy.

I chose the cleaner of the two houses, and then made my way back to the mysterious lady whom I had met at the breakfast table that morning.

I tried to hide my excitement; I badly needed the house, but would it be more than I could afford?

We discussed the situation and I was surprised when I learned that the rent required was only 15 shillings a week. She explained that there would be rates to pay, but she thought that they would be minimal as Cliftonville had not yet recovered from the war damage. Most of the residents had not yet returned, and the chalk cliffs were still framed in barbed wire. Army pill boxes still stood desolate and deserted along the coastline.

We fixed the deal there and then. The agreement being signed, the next step was to send a telegram to my parents to tell them the good news. I needed a few days to recover my furniture from storage, or what was left of it after the Elm Grove episode.

I had saved a little money, enough to buy the necessities, and when all was ready, all I had to do was fetch the children.

At last the war seemed to be drawing to a close. We learned from the press that the Allied Armies were advancing on Berlin from all directions. There were rumours that Hitler was showing signs of madness and had actually tried to eat a carpet in the grip of one of his fits of uncontrollable rage. The other rumours were of death camps for Jews and others. We could not believe it possible and told ourselves that war was a breeding ground for all sorts of rumours.

The next few days were the busiest I have ever encountered, making our new home habitable. There were windows to clean after having been cleared of brown paper, which had to be deluged in hot water and then scraped off.

There were curtains to be made, but because of rationing the only material available was of butter muslin, which I dyed a pale shade of yellow. The paintwork was dingy, so I bought a few cans of apple green paint for the kitchen.

My luck had at last changed and now here I was living near the sea, which I love, the fresh salty air always in my nostrils.

All this good fortune was the result of a journey into the unknown, on a dark joyless night — a journey made without plans, just hope in Divine Providence.

The Almighty did, indeed, guide me that night when I made that journey, alone and a little afraid, to find a home for my husband and children.

CHAPTER
TEN

The Struggle

The war was now drawing to its inevitable conclusion. The Red Army was advancing towards Berlin from the east, eventually to join up in Berlin with the Allied Armies from the west.

Letters from Joe were more frequent, this time from Rome. The troops were having a well-earned rest and there were glowing accounts from Joe, among them one in which he told me of an audience with Pope Pius XII, when he obtained a blessing from the Pope for his brother, who had been ordained a priest.

It seemed certain that it would not be long before my husband would be home again.

Two and a half years had gone by without a husband for me, and a father for Josephine and Kevin.

The following days were spent cleaning, washing paintwork, and attending auction sales or browsing in secondhand shops for an odd wardrobe or armchair.

I still could not afford a washing machine or vacuum cleaner. All washing was done by hand and carpets beaten or swept with a stiff brush. My one luxury was a radio that crackled.

For the garden I bought a spade and a rake, cleared out the weeds and planted some vegetable seeds near the high brick wall that surrounded the garden.

One evening I was digging and came across a small metal object shaped like a butterfly. I gingerly picked it up, instantly realising that it could be a butterfly bomb. I threw it over the wall, expecting to hear a loud explosion, but no sound came. It must have been a dud.

I had seen posters outside the police station describing these objects and warning of the danger.

Although we lived in Cliftonville, one mile from the sea and sandy beaches that skirted the high chalk cliffs, I made a point of taking the children out every day to benefit from the sea air. In winter they would be out in the cold icy winds that blow from the North Pole, and in summer they would bathe or play in the sand or watch the ships pull in to the harbour; consequently they were very healthy, apart from a bout of measles or chickenpox.

When the beaches were crowded it was hard to keep track of them, and to reach home we always had to walk through the park, a lovely spacious area where cricket was played on lazy summer Sunday afternoons.

There was an ornamental garden tucked in a corner, complete with lake and rustic bridge, where we used to sit and listen to the birds or admire the spring flowers, brightening the spirit with their colours.

There were tennis courts, and a café with tables and chairs.

We loved to walk down the pier in summer and watch the passengers come ashore from the old paddle steamers that churned their way from Tower Pier, London, and down the River Thames and along the coast to Margate. They would discharge their happy singing cargoes onto the sands and streets of our town.

Margate was beginning to come to life again. There was never a dull summer moment in the town that slept all winter, when the full force of the icy north wind lashed the shoreline, and many an SOS forced the lifeboatmen from their comfortable beds in the early hours of the morning to go to the aid of a ship floundering on the treacherous Goodwin Sands.

At Christmas, when the snow came, the shops were warm inside and bright with decorations and toys, although waiting for buses or walking home was a cold contrast.

The large hotels started to spring to life with a new coat of paint. There was the Grand or St George's for the more affluent.

As soon as I was reasonably settled, my parents came to stay for a short holiday, to enjoy the bracing air.

They visited the nearby resort of Broadstairs, where Charles Dickens wrote some of his books in Bleak House, which stands on the cliff face as bleak as ever it was.

The quaint harbour of Ramsgate, used in the evacuation of Dunkirk, was within reach, as was Sandwich Bay, where the Vikings had once rowed their long impressive ships before plundering the monasteries for gold chalices, rare paintings, and other valuables.

They visited Dover Castle and discovered the old Pilgrim's Way and on to Canterbury where they saw the magnificence of the Cathedral within a walled city. They saw where Thomas à Becket had been slain in obedience to the King's command, on the steps of the Cathedral Sanctuary.

Margate had everything, from donkey rides on the beach, Punch and Judy shows for the children, to symphony concerts at the Winter Gardens, including the annual Mayoral Ball.

After five years of moving from pillar to post, we were at last beginning to enjoy a measure of stability.

Peace was at last declared. The bells began to chime. Londoners danced in the streets. The Union Jack flew on every building. Even our street was turned into a merry playground for the children. Trestle tables were produced, white table-cloths laid. All the mums set to work to make cakes and sandwiches which were quickly devoured by happy laughing children, all wearing paper hats and tucking into jellies and trifles.

Never had England been so gay and friendly. After tea, races and games were organised for the grown-ups, in which I took part.

The children were soon to see their fathers again.

News came that Joe would be home after being demobilized, issued with a new civilian suit and his War Gratuity.

However, there was a holdup in the homecoming, as the war had left a mark, not physically but mentally. There was a three-week adjustment period needed in a hospital.

CHAPTER
ELEVEN

The Homecoming

The homecoming was arranged for 5th November 1945, which is commonly known as Guy Fawkes Night in England, when people light bonfires and let off fireworks.

When the great day arrived and I had made endless preparations, the children waited all day for their father to appear. Evening came; still no sign of him. I languished around in my most glamorous house gown and finally retired to bed, only to be woken at 1 a.m. by a loud banging at the door. I grabbed my gown, my hair now a tousled mess, my face bereft of makeup, my eyes half open, and opened the door.

It was Joe. We hugged each other, shedding the tears and traumas of two and a half years of separation, hardly realising then how much we both had changed.

At this stage is was too early to assess the changes that had taken place and whether, or how, we could adjust to them. For us, the battle of civilian life was just about to begin.

The attitude of the children to Joe was of love mingled with scepticism. This was a new experience for them; a father to love and to chastise them when necessary, and with the wisdom of children, he had first to prove himself.

The next day was of real acceptance, when we all went off to sample the delights of Dreamland, the fun Mecca of Margate, where they were regaled with candy floss and adorned with balloons after sampling the round-abouts and the ghost train. He came through the test with flying colours as a real live Dad.

We soon found that Margate lacked sufficient industry to employ its returned soldiers, and winter was coming on.

It was around this time that I started to do dressmaking at home, making up garments for a Jewish firm. Meanwhile, all my husband's inquiries for work at the Margate Labour Exchange brought negative results and he was becoming more disillusioned every day. It seemed that after fighting for the country, the country had turned its back on him.

There seemed to be a blanket of post-war malaise settling over Britain. Politically, the people had trusted and lauded our great leader, Winston Churchill — but now they rejected him and chose Clement Attlee to govern the country.

One day, when I was on my way home from shopping, and passing the large garage of a well known car dealer, I noticed a 1931 model Morris car, a stately looking vehicle which was for sale. It was coachbuilt and appeared strong and tough enough to function as a taxi cab. The asking price was £75, exactly the sum of my husband's gratuity.

I had seen more ancient-looking cabs waiting at the taxi rank at Margate Station, although I had no idea of its mechanical condition. On arriving home we discussed the possibilities. If Joe could scrape through the winter months, in the summer we would be laughing all the way to the bank. That was what I optimistically surmised and Joe agreed.

The next day Joe took the old girl for a run. She behaved very well and did all the right things.

She must have been shamming, because thereafter she began to grow tired and expired daily from exhaustion. She could hardly reach the end of the road without breaking down, then a tow truck would be summoned to convey her to the nearest garage, whilst I, gazing out of the front room window, would hold my breath, praying silently: "Oh Lord — keep her going," while my heart sank into my slippers.

Repair bills filled the letter box with monotonous regularity. However, as soon as the phone was connected and an advertisement inserted in the local newspaper, bookings began to roll in.

I had gone to the trouble of making an eye-catching sign to advertise the "Dane Park Taxi Service", but the sign was stolen that night as we slept.

At long last the taxi service was in operation. After her big end had been fixed, her differential adjusted, a nice polish brought up her elegant body, her perfect upholstery cleaned, she began to lose her temperamental character and realise she was there to work and not fool around. After the Christmas holidays and Easter rush from London, we finally became solvent.

My husband, being an extrovert by nature, seemed to enjoy meeting the prospective holidaymakers, taking them to their hotels and making a few tips on top of the fares. There was always plenty of baggage to strap on to the rack at the back of the taxi.

Taxi work was a time consuming job and required my husband's attention from early morning until well after midnight. Once again we became strangers, but at least we could eat, and any spare cash was put in the bank for a rainy day.

On one occasion Joe picked up a well-known theatrical producer who had booked the Theatre Royal, Margate, to put on a play named *The Hasty Heart*. Joe was given complimentary tickets for us to see the play.

After he had described his family, we were all invited to tea with the producer and his wife at their temporary home in Cliftonville, which he had rented for the season.

When summer came we were not exactly laughing all the way to the bank but were able to pay the bills, and, with my extra sewing, things began to work out fairly well.

We changed the Morris and bought an Armstrong-Siddeley. It was a coachbuilt model, built like a battleship and ideal for the taxi business. It was well upholstered and included the luxury of a folding table.

About this time Joe became interested in classical music. Because of the interest, and being on friendly terms with the Borough Librarian, he was invited to present classical recorded symphony concerts in the concert hall of Margate Public Library. He gave these programmes every Friday. There was no admission charge but an expenses collection was taken at the interval. My part in this activity consisted of sketching large portraits of famous composers, which were placed on the wall behind and above my husband's head. He faced the audience sitting at a table with a stack of records, and giving a commentary on the work he was about to play. The room would be bathed in candle light and in winter a large log fire glowed in the fireplace.

One lady came regularly to the programmes with her two spinster sisters. One of them was deaf and always produced a large ear trumpet which she used throughout the programme. Another sister, thrilled with the music if Brahms, inquired of my husband, "Is Brahms still composing?"

"No," came Joe's reply, "I'm afraid he is de-composing."

Early the next spring I had a miscarriage that nearly ended my life. I was having a sea trip on the pleasure boat *Golden Spray* at the time. We were halfway around the bay when it started. The skipper looked worried and insisted on hoisting the distress flag, to summon the ambulance to stand by at the pier, but not wanting to cause a fuss, I said I would be alright if I could lie down in the cabin until we docked and then I would get a taxi home. After I arrived home my husband was summoned, and the doctor.

I awoke in a hospital bed the next day to the sad news that I had lost the baby. I was heartbroken. I had haemorrhaged badly and was given a blood transfusion. My sister came straight away. I am told I did not recognise her. The doctor — a cheerful person — had remarked jokingly, "You redheads always are a problem," meaning that there is a theory in some medical circles that redheads do lose blood more prolifically than brunettes or blondes.

The children were taken to relatives while I spent the next two weeks in hospital, which left me very weak, and it took days before I was able to walk about without feeling dizzy.

My first night at home, my husband was out with the taxi and I began to feel very frightened. I felt as though I was floating out of the window. Whether it was the after effects of the morphine that I had been given every half hour in the hospital, or sheer weakness, I do not know.

I do remember crawling downstairs to the telephone and ringing my husband at the railway station rank. He was away at the time, but someone gave him the message that I was "floating out of the window". He arrived home in a great hurry, thinking it was some sort of a joke and half expecting to see me with wings attached.

I remember the rapturous joy of my first walk up the road and being able to breathe the bracing sea air once again.

As soon as I was reasonably well, the children returned, although I rarely saw my husband. He was fully occupied with the taxi work, especially as the summer months were approaching. I once again took up some work, designing and making dresses for a lady whose husband owned a group of wholesale dress factories.

Although I spent most of my evenings sewing, now and again I would hire a babysitter and go for cycle rides along the coastal roads on summer evenings, at the same time watching the happy groups of holidaymakers enjoying themselves.

I loved spinning down the hills on a June evening when it was light until after 10pm and watching the sun sink in a blaze of red over a calm perfumed sea, the heated earth filling my nostrils with the scent of freshly mown hay.

Cycling had always been my favourite exercise and now it seemed to clear my brain and give me new energy for the tasks ahead.

By this time I had become involved in some church activities, attending monthly meetings. I also found time to join the Thanet Shiplovers Society. I attended talks and went on short sea trips to the Goodwin lightships. We took presents and magazines to the sailors, who led a lonely life, often for many days at a time until relieved by another crew.

On clambering aboard we were deafened by the sound of the bell, which clanged every five minutes in order to warn shipping to steer clear of the treacherous Goodwin Sands. These sands were already studded with the remains of shipwrecks of all descriptions, and mariners give them a wide berth.

Josephine was attending school at Salmestone Grange, a Catholic school built in the grounds of an old monastery. The day came when Kevin joined her. The headmaster told me some of the history of the monastery. It appeared that it was used as a resting place for pilgrims on their way to Canterbury in the early days of Saint Augustine and was the site of an apparition of the Virgin Mary.

In the afternoon I returned to collect the children from school. We visited this church to say a prayer, when my eyes wandered to the old wooden rafters in the roof.

There, distinctly glowing in an aperture at the topmost point of the roof, was a small statue of Our Lady. I immediately asked, "What is a statue of Our Lady doing up there?"

I left the church, quite mystified at the strange phenomenon.

I remember that on his first day at school, Kevin was a naughty boy and refused to behave. His teacher told him that if he played about she would have to smack him. Kevin's reply was classic in the child's view of life: "How could you — a big lady — smack a little boy like me?" She told me that she felt very humbled.

Joe was conspicuous by his absence for most of that summer, but I was determined that as God had given me lovely children, I would enjoy them to the full, although I missed the company of a husband. I had made several good friends and a few acquaintances, but I was beginning to feel like a taxi widow.

However, the children were fed and we had the sea, which I still cherish as my best friend, although one to be respected and even feared.

It was lovely still to have visits from my parents and to watch my father, now 80 years of age, take my five-year-old son for a walk in the park. They would slowly walk down the road as if in deep conversation, stopping every few minutes as if discussing some enormous problem.

Once again, winter was approaching, the holiday-makers thinned out and finally the November fogs hid the sea from view.

The taxi service was barely paying, and Joe had to spend long hours to glean what he could from the local residents, who were now going off on their trips abroad after a good season in their hotels.

The post-war boom for taximen, when holiday visitors threw money around like confetti at a wedding, had all but gone. We just kept our heads above water and that was all.

Joe had a serious breakdown at the Cliftonville house about 1947. The slightest disagreement seemed to disturb the balance of his mind.

On one occasion I was forced to call the police. He began to shout and abuse me, threatening to kill us (although I am sure he never would have done it). He screamed that he hated us all. I asked him if he hated himself. He replied, "Yes!"

I still recall clearly the voice of my five-year-old son Kevin saying. "It's alright Mummy, perhaps he'll love us when we're older."

The next day I sought the help of the Royal Army Service Corps medical officer, as he had rejoined the Army in the last few days. The Officer informed me that he would make it an order that he go for an interview with the Army psychiatrist at Millbank Hospital in London, this being accomplished I was told that my husband was schizophrenic and there was no cure at that time. A week later I saw a solicitor and applied for a legal separation at Margate Magistrates' Court.

When the day came Joe defended the case himself making various accusations against me. The lady magistrate ruled that as we were Catholics we should stay together. She was not a Catholic I found out later. However things improved for a time, further breakdowns were not infrequent but less severe.

CHAPTER
TWELVE

Post-War Blues

The struggle of the early post-war years continued, although we were grateful to God that we had miraculously come through five years of war unscathed. But there was still work to be done. It involved collecting a large bag of dress alterations from a Margate store and returning them completed the following day. It was a case of "Praise the Lord and pass the ammunition"!

I joined the choir at our church, a thing I had not done since my schooldays. It was whilst singing in the choir, I began my second miscarriage. I hastily made some excuse as I left the singers.

After frantic efforts to save the baby by rest and quiet, I landed in hospital. A priest brought Holy Communion as I was very weak from haemorrhaging but still at peace. The thought came to me on this occasion that I could possibly die, but instead of feeling fear, I felt the opposite. There was a feeling of exuberance at the prospect of meeting my Maker.

My ever-loving parents were always near to me. However, after a slow recovery and the warmth of the summer sunshine, I regained my usual strength.

The struggle to keep going with the taxi business had begun to tell on my husband. He smoked rather a lot, although he was not a great drinker.

One night he awoke, hardly able to breathe. His lips became blue and he whispered to me: "Fetch a doctor." I could not use the phone. It had been cut off, as we were unable to pay the account.

It was two o'clock in the morning when I ran to the phone box on the corner and rang the doctor. He answered — sleepily — to my entreaties: "Just give him some brandy and aspirin and I will call in the morning." Luckily, Joe was feeling a little better when I returned, and was going off to sleep again.

Morning came; the doctor arrived. An ambulance was summoned. It was a collapsed lung. There was a slight puncture but no disease.

Joe was not a patient man at the best of times, and, I believe, gave the sisters a rough time, his main worry being that he would not be able to produce the usual Friday evening concert of classical recorded music at the Margate Library.

When Friday morning came, he rose from his sick bed, dressed and told the sister in charge that he was cured. He came home on foot and produced the concert on time, as though he had never been ill at all.

He once again regained full health and not long after I found that I was again pregnant.

It was about this time I received a letter from a very dear school friend stating that she was going to visit the famous Shrine of Fatima, in Portugal, where in the year 1917, some peasant children had seen a vision of the

Holy Mother of God, and where now stands a magnificent church. Would I like to send a petition or written prayer, which she would lay at the Shrine for me?

This I did. I wrote asking the Holy Mother to ask her Son to grant me a healthy living baby.

On 10th April 1948 a beautiful baby girl was born in a Margate nursing home, without complications or fuss. We were delighted with this lovely smiling child. The children loved their new sister. We bought a lovely big pram and took her for many walks in the park or down to the sea.

When the sun was at the front of the house I would park the pram outside the door and as soon as Roberta could sit up, every passer-by received a beaming smile, and I kept a watchful eye from the window.

My next-door neighbour was a frail old lady of genteel stature who had once lived an aristocratic life in the city of Bath, Somerset, but now was reduced to living in the upper part of the house adjoining ours. She came to visit me one afternoon, very distressed.

"My husband is so ill, Mary. I'm waiting for the ambulance, he is in terrible pain with his eyes. Can you come? He likes you so much."

I knew he was blind. I had held his hand when passing him in the street, I could tell he was a gentleman and used to a better way of life.

I rushed into the flat. Yes! He was in agony. There was a big fire in the grate and the room was overbearingly hot, although the day was warm. All the windows were closed.

I immediately opened the windows and heard the sigh of relief. His pain seemed to subside a little and breathing became normal again.

The ambulance arrived and he was taken to hospital. A few days later she called me, this time before breakfast. "Please come in," she asked. "They've brought him back. He died in hospital. He looks so beautiful, so calm."

I had never seen a dead body before, but I had to face it some time, so I braced myself and walked up the stairs, praying for strength.

There, placed in the centre of the room, was a large open coffin containing the body of her husband, a candle at each end. She stood at the head of the coffin smiling, and saying, "There, I told you, Mary, isn't he beautiful?"

I stood in the doorway and then sank to my knees. I could only pray for the repose of his soul, but I feel that I had shared her moment of grief and perhaps lessened the pain.

A month or so later, Joe and I had a long discussion about the taxi business in general. We decided that the sedentary life was detrimental to his health and wellbeing, so we probed the possibility of his rejoining the Army and the healthy life that he had been accustomed to for so many years.

There was a possibility that we would leave our home in Cliftonville and be allocated married quarters in Dover. Army married quarters, I had learnt, were quite comfortable, and included all furniture, bedding and blankets and sheets, china and cutlery, etc.

The pay was regular and the wife's allowance had increased a little. We were still renting our house in Cliftonville, but the owner had since died and she had left the property to a niece, who offered it for sale to us at a low price.

My husband had no money in the bank and I had very little saved, but I hit upon an idea — if it worked, well and good! I would ask the bank for a loan, although I had not even a bank account. The manager was a friendly man. I arranged an interview and outlined my plan to him.

After some thought, the manager agreed to make me a loan of the full amount asked for the house on condition I sold the house within three months and repaid the bank. I reckoned to make a profit of £600 on the deal.

Meanwhile, we were wafted away to Dover to a comfortable married quarter situated at the top of Castle Hill, which was surrounded by a green valley with sloping hills, where cattle grazed in the warm sunshine.

I engaged a solicitor, bought the house, and left the sale in charge of an agent. At last, as the three months were almost over, came the offer I wanted. I sold the house, made my £600 profit, and at last had my first real bank account.

My father had since died of a heart attack at the age of 84, and mother came to stay with us for a short holiday after the funeral.

I think this must have been our most peaceful period, although the strain of the war years, together with the post-war struggle, was still hanging heavily on my husband's head. There were times when he could not stand worry of any kind or even discussion of relevant matters. We loved Dover; the children were free to roam the adjoining fields and watch the cows with their calves, or pick blackberries on the green curves of the encircling hills. I delighted in shopping in Dover or watching the Channel ferry draw in with its cargo of Europeans on holiday. There was so much to see, and the old Castle was one facet of our interest. The children adjusted readily to their new surroundings and schools.

Many happy days were spent in Dover. We now owned a dog and a cat and loved to explore the white cliffs and green slopes.

CHAPTER
THIRTEEN

The White Cliffs of Dover

My mother also enjoyed brief holidays with us and Joe came home every night. We were able to fulfil our long-intended dream to have a fourth child.

The months passed by peacefully, although my husband's nerves were deteriorating somewhat. The smallest worry seemed to be magnified out of all proportion. The trauma of the war years had taken its toll, although at the time I had no idea of the reason.

Although physically stable, he had suffered untold mental harm from his experiences in the front line in the North African and Italian campaigns, for which he received seven medals, including the Coronation Medal of 1937, all consisting of solid silver.

From an extrovert he became an introvert and often suffered melancholia. We began to drift apart, mentally and physically.

This could be the time in most couples' lives when they drift away and contemplate divorce. It seemed that we had come to a stalemate. I had purposely tried to keep myself as attractive as possible, remembering a vow that I had made a few days before our wedding — never to let myself become slovenly in appearance, although my temper, too, was beginning to reach a low ebb. In all the war years and after, we had not really had much time together. However, something kept us together and the expected baby was another happiness for which we thanked God.

The day came when all the signs of the expected birth of our fourth child apparent. I phoned the Army hospital at Shorncliffe. Twenty minutes later an ambulance arrived. It was of the World War One variety and gave me the roughest ride of my life. I arrived at the hospital looking like a boiled red cabbage.

A few hours later Bernard Damien was born, a blond-haired baby boy. After the birth I was wheeled into a ward big enough for 36 people, and realised that I was the only mother there.

As night fell I could hear the laughter of the doctor and the nurse, having fun and games in a distant room. The lights were low, and looking up at the window I saw two faces peering at me.

There were two sets of eyes in the dim light and then scuffling steps as the figures retreated.

I rang the bell at once, summoning the sister, who immediately closed the window.

The children wrote beautiful letters such as this one from Kevin: "Dear Mum: so glad you have a baby. We have a tadpole which is about to change into a frog."

A few days after the homecoming the baby was duly baptised in the Dover Catholic church in the presence of Joe and my mother and the three other children.

The words of the song "The White Cliffs of Dover" had become a reality, and the clouds of war had rolled away.

Not long after Bernard's arrival into the world, we learned of Joe's posting to Canterbury, where he soon found us some modern married quarters. They had three bedrooms and were centrally heated. They were built on top of a hill overlooking the old walled city of Canterbury. We were now accustomed to moving and were looking forward to discovering the joys of this magnificent Cathedral City. We were soon ensconced in our new quarters, complete with dog and cat.

There was a problem with changing schools, but in spite of that Josephine managed to come top of her class with the help of a very fine teacher at the Catholic school in Canterbury.

The house was pleasantly warm in winter and in the spring one felt renewed energy as the beauty of the countryside burst into vibrant colours, woods yellow and blue with primroses and bluebells and trees with their new green leaves. We were fascinated by the narrow streets and quaint Tudor buildings on either side.

The River Stour wound its way, in and out, underneath the overhanging eaves of the quaint buildings with their window boxes of pink geraniums, lending colour to the ancient scenery.

The old ducking chair was still beside the river, once used to quell the tongue of nagging wives. There were quaint cafés where one ate cottage teas with fresh scones and cream.

At the other end of the city were the modern shops where one could buy any variety of goods, including the most exclusive shoes and couture dresses.

In the summer evenings when my husband was home, I was able to wander on my bicycle, free to enjoy the rambling country lanes and the gardens of the thatched roofed cottages.

When Bernard was six months old I received a letter from my mother saying that she had not been feeling too well. I was alarmed and rang her the same day, stating that Joe could get compassionate leave and I would come straight away.

Independent as always, she insisted that I should not do so, saying she was feeling a little better.

A week later I received a telegram: "Come at once. Mother ill." It was Josephine's 12th birthday. I rang my husband and left at once, but when I arrived it was too late.

I was greeted at the door by the nuns from the convent where her sister had been for some years. "She has gone," they said. I was stunned. My aunt told me that my mother had died peacefully one hour before I arrived.

I looked at the face of my mother until the nuns led me away.

I had with me Bernard, who was demanding his breast feed and a nappy change. Life had to go on. I could only pray for the soul of my mother.

I spent a night alone in the house with a fractious baby and the body of my mother at rest in the back room. The nuns had gone back to the convent and I felt very much alone that night.

Next day there was the funeral to arrange, and my sister and her husband arrived from Ireland, making things a little easier.

The funeral was held in the church of Saint Thomas More at Eastcote, where my husband and I had been married.

CHAPTER
FOURTEEN

On the Move Again!

It was two weeks later when the shock of my mother's death really hit me. I just cried all night until there were no more tears.

When my mother's will was eventually finalised, my half share enabled me to buy the few luxuries I had so long gone without, such as a vacuum cleaner and refrigerator. The rest I invested.

Fulfilling the unusual pattern of our lives, we were seen to follow my husband to his next posting, which was to be near Yeovil in Somerset, to inhabit a comfortable and well designed married quarter at a place called Houndstone, a few miles from Yeovil. There were grassy lawns outside each three-bedroomed house, and every home boasted a large back garden.

When we were settled in, Joe was able to resume his classical recorded symphony concerts, this time in the YMCA Hall. The concerts were very successful and appealed to quite a large number of Army personnel and civilians from Yeovil who came to the programmes.

We were able to buy a Hillman saloon car, and I had hoped to learn to drive. Josephine minded the children while Joe took me through the rudiments of driving. In this case, the "rudiments" were extremely rude.

It was a Saturday I won't forget in a hurry when I took the wheel. The big "L" plate was tied to the car, and off we started. I drove fairly well, as I thought, down the winding lanes. My husband's temper became more frayed as I ground the gear box once or twice, until he finally exploded, his face crimson with rage.

It was more than I could stand. Finally, in exasperation I said, "Look — I won't stay in this car while you are in a temper." I got out of the car. To my astonishment, he drove off, leaving me 10 miles out in the country with only a few shillings in my pocket.

I started to walk home and walked five miles until I came to a bus route, waiting on the lonely roadside for an hour until the bus arrived. It terminated at Yeovil outside a cinema.

I was so exhausted I staggered in to see the film and arrived home at nearly midnight with a large blister on my foot, only to see my husband blissfully sitting in his armchair reading the newspaper. I was too tired to talk or argue and went to bed feeling pretty disgusted.

How can one leave four children? I could have walked out, never to return.

After that I used the services of a driving instructor, only to fail on a technical point.

* * *

The children loved Somerset. It was the home of my late mother's father, who hailed from a little village called Shepton Mallet, which we decided to visit, inquiring if there were any of my relatives still living there. Sure enough, we found a Miss Shepherd living in a quaint old cottage in the centre of the village.

She was a dear old lady with white hair, and although we arrived unannounced, we were invited to have tea, which consisted of a large spread of cucumber sandwiches and homemade cakes and scones. There was a cheerful log fire burning in the open grate and we were able to tell the dear lady news about her family.

We left, promising to write, and thanked her for the lovely reception she had provided for us.

The children would take long walks, bringing back posies of wild flowers which they proudly presented to me.

One night we had retired when the baby awoke and started crying. I went to the bathroom to get some powder when I heard a "thud, thud" like footsteps by the downstairs window, and with the light from the bathroom clearly saw the startled face of a man gazing at me.

"What are you doing there?" I yelled. He jumped over the fence and disappeared. I summoned my husband, but it was impossible to wake him. We reported the incident to the military authorities next day.

We loved the quaint country inns of Somerset, our favourite being the "Headless Woman". Outside the inn was a large sign with a woman carrying her head under her arm. I loved to hear the people speak in the pleasant drawling dialect and absorb their philosophy of life.

Unfortunately, the day would come when Joe's service with the RASC (Royal Army Service Corps) would be at an end. We would then need a home of our own. It was decided that as most of our friends lived on the East Kent coast and more industry had come to that area, it would be wise to buy a house there before the prices started to rise, London being too expensive and too crowded.

When Joe came home on leave I decided to look for a permanent home and with the money from my mother's will was able to put down a deposit on a five-bedroomed house in Kingsgate, halfway between Broadstairs and Cliftonville, in Kent. It was well built and had a long garden with fruit trees.

The sea was only five minutes' walk away and there was a bus at the top of the avenue to shopping areas.

Joe remained in Somerset, although on his next leave he took us to Kingsgate in the Hillman, where we soon settled in.

The children went back to their respective schools and I took a job for the winter in Bobby's, one of a chain of exclusive seaside resort stores, though it was imperative that I had to leave Bernard at the nursery school each day, although I hated doing it.

I worked as a dress fitter attached to the showroom. We were a happy crowd and often convulsed with laughter.

There was the lady in the millinery department who had once been an opera singer and was known as the "Melba of the Midlands" for her powerful singing voice. She had the very large bust with which female opera singers are usually endowed. I was once invited to hear her sing at the hostel where she was staying, and I stood near the piano. "Don't stand there, my dear," she urged, "you will get all the blast." She was right — she nearly shattered the windows.

After a while I tried the bed and breakfast idea. It worked for one summer.

The next year I decided to do dress alterations at home. I had cards printed and posted, one in each letter box. Soon the neighbours were providing me with plenty of work and I could keep an eye on the children.

On one occasion, a dear old lady of 91 summoned me to her large house. She told me it was her companion's day off. She pointed to a large cardboard box which, she said, had not been opened for 50 years. She wished to open it in my presence.

Taking off the lid, it was like a journey into the past. I removed the yellow tissue paper, uncovering the most beautiful handmade lace wedding gown, but yellow with age. There was a faded tulle veil, a fan, and some long kid gloves.

I wished that I could have waved a wand and restored the contents of the box together with her lost youth, and I regretted being unable to touch the lace without the threads disintegrating.

We placed the gown safely away, perhaps for another 50 years.

CHAPTER
FIFTEEN

From Cold to Hot

The following day there was a letter from Joe to say that he was being posted to Singapore for three years. If we wanted to come he could apply for married quarters and a passage on a ship.

Once again, the children would be uprooted from their schooling but it seemed the natural thing for us to do. It would mean having to let the house, so it was not long before I had some tenants, an American family stationed at Manston Airbase. They needed to move in almost immediately and we had to find temporary accommodation.

I applied to Army headquarters and after a lot of urgent phone calls and letter writing, the Army decided to send us to a Transit Camp near Liverpool, in the north of England. To us, it was just another move.

I packed a large laundry hamper with clothes which were sent on in advance. We carried two large suitcases and proceeded north. It was January and freezing cold.

Our destination was on the outskirts of Liverpool, a place named Maghull, which the children quickly named "Mughole". It was snowing when we arrived. The Army hut was clean but lacked home comforts. There was an iron stove at one end and a bundle of sticks with which to start a fire. I sent Kevin to get some coal and on the way he was met by a friendly woman who gave him a bunch of flowers and said: "Here you are, love — make the place less like a concentration camp." He smiled and thanked her.

We soon had a fire going and sat around warming ourselves. To our horror, we were not alone. There, as cheeky as anything, was a small mouse with the same idea. He had extra large ears, possibly listening to our conversation, but we soon got rid of him.

While waiting for news of our sailing date, and rather than sit all day in the hut in Mughole, we decided to use every minute to the best advantage. The next two weeks we spent riding on the top deck of the double decker bus into Liverpool to see the sights. There was the famous dock railway, now demolished to make way for new buildings, and the magnificent Art Gallery where we lingered over the beautiful works of art. The market was also a fascinating attraction, where we bought our Sunday joint of meat.

We had to set aside one day for inoculations, and had some difficulty finding the Army Medical Centre on a very foggy day in a strange city.

At long last the letter arrived giving details and a list of instructions. I had already signed numerous forms and now we were to sail in the P&O liner SS *Canton* from Southampton early in February.

Again the bags were packed and we boarded the train to London, and thence to Southampton.

Once on board my worries seemed to fade away. I knew that this was going to be the trip I had dreamed about.

Our cabin steward was an elderly Goanese, who kept a fatherly eye on the children and gave them the discipline they needed.

Josephine was now 16 years of age and already blossoming into a beautiful young girl.

The next three years were even more eventful, but this time the struggles were over and living became real fun.

PART TWO

Three Years in Singapore

CHAPTER
SIXTEEN

Ship Ahoy

Like sunshine after rain, we watched our troubles drift away through the portholes of the 16,000-ton SS *Canton*. The snow-covered coastline of southern England became slowly dimmer on that ice-cold morning in February 1956. We loved England, had suffered with her in her time of trouble. We now listened to a new sound which featured in our daily lives until we reached Singapore. It was the throbbing of the turbines which drove the engines of our floating home, and the splashing of the waves on the bows that became music to our ears.

The children lost no time in finding their way around the ship. Each came back offering tit-bits of information, like "special agents" in our private "network". Kevin had found a new friend and Roberta had stolen the heart of an elderly musician, now cut off from his own home and family. Josephine had her eye on a good-looking officer, and Bernard had gone off his food. Four responsibilities for four weeks and four reasons for living and loving.

Every day I studied the ship's chart and it was not long before we reached the Bay of Biscay. We had already practised our lifeboat drill, found our sea legs, and had retired to our cabins.

It was the third night at sea. The children were asleep in their bunks when suddenly the lights failed and the turbines stopped throbbing. We seemed to be drifting like a ghost ship on silent water. I looked at my watch. It was 2.30 a.m. and I eagerly waited for an announcement. Not a sound was heard. I looked towards the lifebelts — just in case!

I grabbed my rosary, prayed without waking the children, and listened to the waves splashing against the porthole.

My thoughts wandered back in history to my paternal grandfather, Captain John Algernon Sydney, owner of his own square-rigged ship, *Master Mariner*, and educated at the Naval College, Greenwich. His ship was wrecked in the Bay of Biscay at possibly the same degree of latitude and longitude. I said a prayer for his soul.

After what seemed to be an eternity, the lights came on and the turbines commenced their merry tune.

On making inquiries next day, I learned that it was a breakdown in the electrical supply system, possibly God jerking my brain and reminding me not to forget Him in the good times as well as the bad.

Soon we steamed through the Straits of Gibraltar. A few days later the climate changed and the days became warm and sunny. We could see the Atlas Mountains of North Africa, snow-capped and sweeping in rugged lines to the Mediterranean. Then Algiers came into view, a cluster of white domes nestling between bare deserted mountains. By night we passed Malta — the sky reminiscent of diamonds sparkling on a cushion of black velvet.

By this time the passengers had recovered from the effects of *mal de mer* and had begun to join the land of the living. One lady was a missionary returning to Malaya, another was a doctor's widow trying to overcome the loss of her husband.

It was midnight when we drifted into Port Said under a black velvet sky. Our first introduction to the Middle East was the "phut-phut" sound of the motor boats as they brought fresh water to the thirsty ship.

After daybreak we were treated to a brilliant sunrise which embraced the earth, sea, and sky with red and gold; then exotic aromas began to fill our nostrils.

Suddenly we were invaded from all sides as native merchants climbed aboard with their wares. We inspected the goods.

"You buy," they persisted — "very cheap." Leather bags, camel saddles, cigars.

"You got plenty money?" they inquired, to which we replied emphatically, "No."

After breakfast we went ashore to inspect the shops, laden with the most beautiful handworked goods, and perfumes from Paris.

We were glad to leave this bustling hive of activity and glide slowly along the Suez Canal. It was like being on top of the world as we stood high on deck overlooking vast areas of desert with, here and there, a pyramid or a green oasis.

Our next port of call was Aden, where goats wandered freely in the dusty streets and veiled women walked in twos or threes.

After a morning spent viewing the duty free goods in the open fronted shops, we were glad to return to the ship for a shower and a good lunch, then share our experiences with the other passengers.

After lunch I found a quiet corner on deck and relaxed near the swimming pool while the Red Sea tossed the ship gently. I shut my eyes and pondered on the joy of being alive.

Suddenly, a pillow was thrust behind my head, a stool placed under my feet, a pair of sunglasses placed over my eyes. Looking up, I noticed a tall, good-looking young man had seated himself opposite to me. At least it was a novel way of introduction. I thanked him for all the attention he was bestowing on me and learned that he was a Scotsman returning to a rubber plantation in Malaya to take over from his father, and that his friend seated beside him was a tin mining engineer also stationed in Malaya. They were both returning from leave in Cairo.

I hardly dared to say that I was a soldier's wife, bound for Singapore to join my husband. However, it soon became obvious with the return of the children from their various activities.

My female friends arrived and we were all invited to a shipboard party that evening.

The decks were arranged with coloured lanterns, the moon came up to add romance to that unforgettable night somewhere in the Red Sea. We danced until dawn and discussed happy and serious events in our lives. The tin miner was still grieving for a friend shot by the Communists in the jungles of Malaya. He sadly showed me the press cutting. The Scotsman, after a few drinks, was eulogising on the advantages of being Scottish. The soldier's wife whom I had befriended was now gazing into the eyes of the tin miner. It was early morning when I retired after a wonderful evening of dancing and fun.

After breakfast the children told me they had seen flying fish, so we all peered overboard to get a glimpse of these bird-like sea creatures swimming in the water.

The children were so busy with deck games, while Bernard played in the nursery, that I only saw them at meal times. The nights were beautifully serene, with Arabia on our port side and the moon looming above. I thought of that lovely poem of Walter de la Mare: "Far are the Shades of Arabia — where the princes ride at noon — mid the verduous forests and thickets — under the ghost of the moon."

CHAPTER
SEVENTEEN

Singapore Bound

Bombay was soon reached and the dockside bustled with activity. The Tamil labourers walked in single file, carrying bales of merchandise head high, their long ebony limbs shining against the white of their cotton loincloths. Graceful Indian ladies swathed in saris of silk, interwoven with gold thread, paraded to and fro.

We went ashore and hailed a taxi, our first stop being the Taj Mahal Hotel, a symphony in good taste with its red-carpeted staircase, wrought iron balustrade and white marble floors.

We visited the grand arch known as the "Gateway to India", the hanging gardens and a Buddhist temple. At this stage the taxi driver told us the fare would be double the price we had agreed to, so we decided to return to the ship, at the same time noticing many beggars lying in the crowded streets and the trams with their windows covered with wire mesh, telling a story of past violences.

Our next port of call was Ceylon, now called Sri Lanka, where we visited the Cinnamon Gardens and the museum, where we saw a party of Buddist monks wearing saffron robes and carrying begging bowls. We were invited to a jeweller's shop and were permitted to try on rings worth thousands of dollars, rubies, emeralds and sapphires, all sparkling and beautiful.

Soon we were back on board preparing for our next shore visit, but before we arrived all sorts of preparations had been made for fun and dancing, including a fancy dress dance in which the children also took part. I became Nell Gwyn for one night and carried a basket of oranges, kindly donated by the chef. Josephine was a jockey, Roberta a flapper of the 1920s, Bernard a pirate and Kevin a sheikh. It was gala night and the dining room was tastefully decorated for the occasion.

That night I danced with the Captain, a stockily built man, the Purser, a tall, plump cheerful person, and the Chief Engineer, an older man with greying hair and firm countenance. The sea was calm, the sky electric with stars and the moon glowing like a huge balloon in the night sky.

The next few days were spent gazing out to sea, watching eagerly for the coast line of Malaya, where Penang was our next port of call. We were greeted by gentle Asian fishermen seated in frail boats or *prahus*.

In the distance was a palm-fringed shore with a background of misty mountains covered in dense jungle growth. We were dazzled by the whiteness of the Government buildings, surrounded by vivid green lawns. Here and there stood the tall flame of the forest and frangipani trees, their branches covered in waxy white perfumed blossom, intoxicating the senses.

We visited the waterfall gardens, a tropical paradise where the sky is hidden by fronds and creepers that trail to the ground.

We seemed to be in another world, wherein is heard the ceaseless cacophony of unseen musicians. Suddenly, monkeys sprang out in all directions, amusing the children with their antics.

After the heat of the day Josephine and I were invited to the Mariners' Club, where we sipped cold drinks and reclined in comfortable chairs, the children safely tucked up aboard ship, with Vaz — our Goanese cabin steward — keeping a watchful eye on them.

Penang was pregnant with excitement, for it was the Chinese New Year celebration and the colourful dragon was paraded throughout the city. Fireworks crackled as the young men performed their fiery dance.

My daughter and I were invited by the ship's officers to attend a Malay dance in the town on this festive evening. To get to the attap-built hall, we availed ourselves of the passing tri-shaws, and soon arrived at the dimly lit dance hall. We entered and began joining in the Malay version of sambas and rumbas until it was time to return to the ship, for, like Cinderella, we had to be back before midnight, when she would sail for Singapore.

In the rush to return, we found a crowd of people with shocked expressions. Someone had been stabbed outside the hall. We managed to grab a taxi and were back just in time, only to learn that sailing time had been extended by one hour.

The next few days aboard were spent watching the emerald green of the coastline.

We visited the engine room in order to appease Kevin's curiosity. A door was opened for us on the main deck and a gust of hot air blew in our faces. There in front of us was an iron spiral staircase which we descended into the bowels of the ship. We were greeted by two engineers wielding oil cans, who pointed out the mechanics of the ship to Kevin, but I found it all too bewildering and was glad to retreat to the cool deck before fainting with the heat.

Our destination was at last being realised. Bernard was excited and smiling at the thought of seeing his Dad; in fact the whole ship was agog with excitement as passengers made their farewells.

The gangway was placed in position. As people began to leave the ship I felt a pang of envy for those continuing to Hong Kong. Oh well! *C'est la vie*. Only the French have words to explain the unexplainable.

We searched for a tall man, six foot three inches, and it wasn't until nearly everyone had left that he arrived, explaining that he had been arranging for an Army car to take us to our new home.

We had eight miles to travel, past rubber plantations, attap huts — past Malays in colourful sarongs and Chinese girls in their cheongsams; a whole new world of exciting sounds and new fragrances.

CHAPTER
EIGHTEEN

A New Way of Life

Our new home in Singapore was a gleaming white, three-bedroomed bungalow built of brick and plaster and situated in Serangoon Garden Estate.

It boasted a large front garden with double wrought iron gates and had large windows which were heavily barred.

Each room had a large ceiling fan as it was imperative to keep the windows open day and night, and the bars were there for safety, although most Singapore houses had their window grilles designed in artistic patterns.

We were now foreigners in this new country, although it was administered by the British Government. There was a definite undercurrent of feeling for self-rule, or "Merdeka" as it was called in Malay.

This young and polyglot race was passionately seeking to become more independent each day, although surprisingly enough there were considerably few differences of opinion

Every day one encountered Malays, Chinese, Indians (of all castes), tall Sikhs, hardworking Tamil labourers and some Eurasians. The atmosphere in the shopping centres was friendly and extremely polite.

In some instances where a Chinese had lost face, I had seen two attempted stabbings, as tempers run hot in the tropical atmosphere. The sun shone almost continuously, then rain would fall for about ten minutes every morning and the sun reappeared, giving way to a Turkish bath atmosphere, with clouds of steam rising from the scorched ground.

During the monsoon period from October to December, roads became rivers, with water pouring into the six-foot-wide open drains which, in turn, became swirling torrents flowing uninterrupted to the larger creeks, and finally the sea.

The nights cooled down a little, so that our evenings were usually spent seated on the patio listening to the music and the sound of the cicadas.

We were never pestered by mosquitoes, thanks to the small lizard-like creatures that would climb our walls and run along the ceiling, held only by suction pads on their feet. Their long tongues would reach out and demolish any insect that dared to enter our home. These friendly creatures were known as "Chic Chacs" and never seemed to intrude on the furniture or bedding.

The only dread of our lives were the cockroaches, which were kept down by spraying the dark corners once a day with a well-known product.

Our *amah*, a plump Cantonese lady of about 40, was allocated to us by the Army, to do our laundry and housework. She had a beaming smile and a mouthful of gold teeth. Her shiny black hair was tied into a pigtail. She always wore a white oriental blouse and wide black trousers.

Although we grew to love Gwey Sing, we could never quench her desire to starch everything in sight, so much so that often it was painful for Kevin to sit down in his cotton shorts.

Many hawkers toured the estate in the course of the day, one being the "mah-mee-man" who would appear at the brow of the hill beating on a bamboo stick to summon customers to taste the Chinese food which he prepared with a flourish at the kerbside, using a large wok on a charcoal stove. He served the odorous concoction on a large leaf.

The next to appear was the Chinese broomseller, virtually enveloped in brooms, brushes, and feather dusters. Not even his head was visible. The brooms hung from a pole slung across his bronzed shoulders. Shortly after, the Indian balloon man arrived; he was enveloped with balloons of all colours, so that only his bandy brown legs could be seen.

Children appeared from all directions, including Bernard, who rushed out excitedly to procure a balloon.

In spite of the heat, I found Gwey Sing had a unique way of making the beds by jumping over the beds from one side to the other. I suppose it's quicker than walking round them. She loved children and was always on hand to babysit if necessary. We really became fond of her and treated her as one of the family.

All our shopping was done at the Cold Storage Store. The market, though cheaper, was suspect. So many people handled the meat, it began to stink.

Buying tropical fruit was quite an event. There were so many varieties, except, of course, for the durian, which had such a strong unpleasant odour that natives claimed that it could be smelt from one mile away. However, the inside of the fruit was delicious.

CHAPTER
NINETEEN

Getting Acclimatised

After a month had passed, we slowly became accustomed to the rhythm of life in Singapore and were only mildly astonished when we were awakened early in the morning by our neighbours screaming and moaning at the top of their voices. My first thought was that the whole family had taken poison.

At 6am my husband was dressed and prepared to go to his Army duties at Pasir Panjang. The children were ready for their school bus which departed at 7am, for they were due back at 1.30pm. Gwey Sing arrived, and prepared to plunge into her task of washing and cleaning, and by making signs to her I was able to imply that I was puzzled by the noise emanating from the house next door. Just then, the grocer boy arrived and was able to give us some information. It appeared that in the night a man had died. He was Tiong Choon, the wealthy owner of a string of grocer shops, a bus company and a revered member of one of Singapore's secret societies. Paid mourners had been called in to wail and scream. From that moment onward the neighbour's house became a hive of activity which lasted for a week.

A large roughly hewn coffin arrived from a truck

parked outside, and our conversation was interrupted by the loud hammering of nails being driven into the solid wood. Cars and trucks arrived, bringing Chinese people of every age, some covered from head to foot in sackcloth, their waists tied with string. These sombre figures filed through the one-storey house to pay their respects to the dead man.

Children played merrily outside while men prepared to make altars to Buddha, one against the outer wall of the house, and one directly above the monsoon drain against the front fence. A large brightly coloured backdrop was placed behind the altar, garishly reminiscent of an English fairground.

Joss sticks were burned and the air became saturated with incense and the smell of roast pork, which the amahs were busily preparing in the back garden in order to feed the hungry mourners. A real life drama had begun to unfold and this was Act One.

More trucks began to arrive, bringing an array of banners, each inscribed with Chinese characters. These were placed around the perimeter of the garden. Large joints of pork were carried into the house, together with numerous crates of orange drinks.

The next trucks to arrive brought the musicians, who deafened us with the clashing of cymbals in a wild, ferocious rhythm and filled the road with thunderous vibrations. The Chinese belief was that the loud noise would keep the evil spirits at bay.

Although Tiong Choon slept peacefully, there wasn't much sleep for the inhabitants of Serangoon the whole of that week.

Gwey Sing was a little jealous, the grocer boy told me. She say, "Rich man have big funeral, but a poor person is buried next day."

As I strolled up the road in the evening, I noticed arc lamps had been trained on the house of death. My children were fascinated by the gay balloons and pieces of Christmas tinsel attached to the altar. There were bowls of rice and fruit placed in front of the deity.

Hundreds of small round chairs and tables were placed in the front garden and laid out for a feast. The road was soon impassable because of parked cars. Armed police arrived to control the crowds. More trucks arrived, each bringing at least 30 men who took their places at the tables. As evening drew near, the only sound was the clearing of throats and the clatter of mahjong chips as the men played throughout the night.

There must have been about 150 men in the next door garden that night, although they were amazingly quiet. We still had to shut our windows and turn the ceiling fan on full blast.

Six am arrived too soon and the men began to return to their homes and to their respective jobs.

The whole scene was re-enacted each night for a week, until the funeral on the following Sunday, when Act Two began to unfold, bringing new surprises.

CHAPTER
TWENTY

The Melting Pot

The next day I needed a diversion and decided to take Bernard into the busy metropolis of Singapore. The bus was crowded with Chinese women wearing neatly starched samfoos, their shiny black hair coiled on the nape of the neck. They were going to market, obviously to sell a duck or two, as from under the seat came the "quack quack" of a duck, as a narrow beak protruded appealingly from each basket. Bernard was delighted and declared: "Look — it's Donald Duck."

Chinese girls were seated demurely dressed in cheongsams. Next to Bemard was a tall Indian, who gazed down at his fair skin and occasionally stroked his blond hair while Bemard smiled awkwardly.

The bus rattled along the dusty road, past the Malay kampongs and the open-fronted shops of the Chinese and Indian merchants. We looked up at the names. There was Mee Sin, the dentist, next door, Sin Mee, the tailor, there was Ah So, Ah Fat, and Poo Me. We came to a large poster advertising a patent medicine guaranteed to cure piles and eyes.

The Malay driver halted the bus suddenly, having careered at top speed for the last ten minutes. The reason for the jolt was the appearance of a trishaw rider from nowhere. A few choice Chinese words were exchanged, but nothing seemed to perturb the comely Malay woman with five plump little children seated around her. The odour of curry heralded our approach to the Indian quarter, the shops gay with coloured saris and other silks. There were paper flowers and exotic leis of frangipani flowers.

An Indian clad in a loincloth was seated on the counter, a string attached to his toe holding a lei in position, while he threaded ribbon in and out between the flowers.

Next door an Indian was sitting cross-legged on the counter amongst the confectionery, filling bags with brightly coloured sweets. We noticed tall Sikhs, their white turbans enhancing their handsome bearded faces and dignified demeanour, going about their business of money lending.

The sari-clad women wore a red spot on the forehead or a diamond in their nose to denote class.

Singapore was well known as the "Melting Pot of the East". I learned that about 6,000 BC ancestors of the Australian aboriginals had passed through the swampy land on their island-hopping migration to new homes.

Singapore had felt the influence of the Malays, Chinese, Indians, Javanese, and finally the British, until having achieved their own freedom.

As we approached the city we passed the Government buildings, their pillars rising tall and stately, and saw the brilliant green padang, the scene of many former assemblies, pageants and cricket matches telling of a bygone era. It was here that on 28th January 1819 an Englishman — Thomas Stamford Raffles — had landed, and was greeted by 150 fisherfolk.

Our bus journey came to an end and the whole Singapore waterfront unfolded before us — the third largest harbour in the world. Bernard craned his neck to look at the numerous ships anchored in the bay and beyond to the pale outlines of the Javanese Islands. We were soon swallowed up into the jaws of the throbbing metropolis.

When Sunday came, we prepared to go to Mass at Seletar, an Air Force base only five miles distance from our home. We piled into the Vauxhall car that my husband had bought and drove past vivid green vegetation. The roads were lined with tall coconut palm trees, their leaves swaying like silver swords in the tropical breeze.

Buffalo sauntered down to the still pools of water. Natives, naked to the waist, splashed themselves at the roadside water taps. Smiling Malay children waved a greeting as we passed.

A party of Malay boys appeared, exquisitely dressed in sarongs of deep purple made of hand-loomed pure silk and richly interwoven with silver thread. Their shirts were white and a songkok, or velvet hat, shaped like a fez lent dignity and height to their medium stature. They smiled charmingly, exposing gleaming white teeth, and we waved to them.

The church was light and airy, although outside the sun was brilliant and the heat intense. The Mass was well attended by Army and Air Force personnel and their wives and children.

After the service we were offered a cool drink in an adjoining room, chatted with the other families and then wound our way home.

On returning to Serangoon we found that the gate in our entrance way was blocked by a procession of cars decorated with banners and scrolls. Hundreds of people were congregating in the street, many carrying yellow umbrellas, although it was not raining. We learnt that these signified the particular Tong or Secret Society of which the deceased had been a member. A mah-mee seller was also doing a roaring trade outside our garden gate.

After a while we were able to clear the driveway of people, grab a cool drink and sit on the patio and watch the Grand Finale of the funeral ceremony.

Next to arrive were four large trucks containing the musicians. Each band was hired by the four sons of the dead Tiong Choon and performed while the musicians were still seated in the back of the truck. The music was the wild clashing of cymbals, almost barbaric in intensity, but fascinating.

From the late Tiong Choon's residence, women appeared with objects made of coloured paper — boats, houses, aeroplanes. They set fire to the replicas one by one, believing that these articles would accompany the departed spirit on his journey into the after-life.

While the final band played, a large truck arrived covered in garish decorations. Blue and gold cloth was draped from the sides of the truck into a central dome-shaped canopy, and a large photo of the deceased was placed on the bonnet. The truck driver was having a little doze and was sprawled out comfortably under the canopy until, hearing the approach of the mourners with the coffin, he sprang to his feet to take his place at the steering wheel. The mourners filed in procession following the coffin, moaning and wailing in unison, dressed in their sackcloth, their heads covered by hoods. The coffin was placed in position under the canopy. The truck drew away and the procession began to wind its way slowly to the cemetery, and Serangoon was once again restored to its usual peace and quiet.

CHAPTER
TWENTY-ONE

The Wedding Feast

On the Monday after the funeral we were visited by a representative of the Army authorities, who took note of our accommodation and decided that we were entitled to a larger house, according to the size of our family. It was subsequently arranged that we would be moved to another house on the Serangoon Garden Estate.

This one was larger and had three upstairs bedrooms, a bathroom and toilet, large lounge and adjoining kitchen. The furniture was of simple design in light teak, the floors tiled and covered with Indian carpet.

The new home was soon shipshape, but the children felt that it was not complete without a dog. So a visit was made to the dogs' home. We surveyed the array of abandoned dogs and one in particular seemed to plead "take me home". It was a ginger, smooth-haired mongrel with intelligent brown eyes. We made our choice and named the new member of the family "Kim".

It was interesting to discover the attitudes of the different races to the dog.

The Malays believe dogs to be unclean and will never pat one. Should they come in contact with the animal, they must wash their hands immediately.

The Chinese believe that the dog carries the spirit of a bygone ancestor.

We began to make friends with the people of Singapore, one of whom was a Chinese interpreter who worked in my husband's office at Pasir Panjang. He was a plump, amiable and highly intelligent man, and from him we received a printed invitation to the wedding feast of his eleventh brother. We were delighted to accept and took our daughter, Josephine, with us.

The feast was held on the top floor of a modern square building.

Mr and Mrs Chen were there to receive the guests and ushered us into a large hall where 100 Chinese people were seated at round tables. We were placed next to a cousin of our friend and some English officers from Pasir Panjang. We were then treated to an eleven-course meal which was interrupted after the sixth course with bowls of scented water and muslin cloths with which to cool our hands and faces.

The first dish to arrive was placed in the centre of the table. We took a small portion with our chopsticks. The menu consisted of:

1. Seven stars with the moon
2. Edible bird's nest soup
3. Shark's fin à la Mandarin
4. Roast chicken
5. Fried abalone
6. Roast suckling pig
7. Prawn fritters
8. Steamed pomfret

9. Fish stomach soup
10. Fried rice
11. Fruits and desserts

We tasted each dish and found them delicious.

Every guest was in a merry mood when the ancient custom of the bridegroom feeding the bride from a baby's bottle, and vice versa, was taking place. We were told that this was a good luck symbol.

After the enjoyable feast the officers invited us to a party, but my husband thought it best to return home as he had to be up early in the morning.

CHAPTER
TWENTY-TWO

A New Job

The children needed new clothes, I needed a sewing machine and Josephine needed a typewriter for her commercial course.

There was only one thing to do, and that was to look for some kind of work. Not being commercially minded, there were only one or two jobs of which I was capable. Sewing! There were too many dressmakers already.

Although I had never sold clothes before, I was sure I could do it. There was one likely boutique where I would inquire if they needed a saleslady. It was the boutique attached to the famous and historic Raffles Hotel. Every time I passed this shop I knew that this was where my interests lay, although I hardly had the courage to confront the owner.

Many times I peered inside the entrance, with its beautiful wrought iron gates that led from Bas Basah Road to the shop. Inside was an Aladdin's cave of delights, the rich deep reds of the Persian carpets on the white tiled floor, the mother-of-pearl embossed Chinese screens and the glow from small table lamps against the mirrored walls.

It was some time before I plucked up the courage to walk in and ask to see the couturier, who was Doris Geddes, an Australian lady from Sydney.

Suitably attired in a simple well-cut dress, I walked in and asked for an interview.

I was more than surprised when Mrs Geddes told me that she was looking for someone to help Tina, the lovely Chinese girl who had worked there for many years.

Mrs Geddes was going abroad. Tina and I would be alone except for a friend, a Singapore judge's wife who would call in occasionally to do the book-keeping and banking. "It is important that you get on well together," she declared. Tina was a charming person, very slim and beautifully dressed in a silk cheongsam with high side slits, revealing shapely legs. She knew the wealthy clients and was talented at blending colours.

Swee Ching was the young assistant, who walked like a queen, her hair held back in a pony tail which swayed on her delicate shoulders. The amah, Ah Choy, was plump, and bustled about wielding a feather duster. There were two tailors who were lovingly named Fat Tailor and Thin Tailor. They worked in an air-conditioned workroom at the rear of the hotel.

Fat Tailor sported one long whisker that reached down from his chin to his fat, round stomach. Thin Tailor — I was told — smoked opium occasionally, hence the sweet sickly odour from his yellow skin.

My duties were normally 9am to 5pm, except when the tourist ships arrived and then it was 11.30am to 9pm.

Having made arrangements for the children to be well looked after, I began my duties at the Raffles Hotel boutique. My first days were spent getting acquainted with the contents of this unique and magnificent collection of articles. There were hand-loomed silks of every jewel shade from Bangkok, fine silk gauze from Peking, hand-loomed pure silk brocade from China, dresses made from saris and sarongs.

The tables were of Louis XIV period, with here and there a table lamp from Paris or an article of jade or amber. There were fitting rooms at the rear and a room with long racks of imported gowns, and gowns made from hand-blocked batik sarongs.

Folding glass doors led out on to a patio, shady with creepers, where there were marble tables on which were placed silver candlesticks. Many well-known people visited the shop from all over the world while staying in the Raffles Hotel. It was whilst sitting alone one evening on the swinging divan, after Tina had gone home, that I was conscious of someone standing behind me, although I had not heard any footsteps approaching.

I looked up suddenly, to find the tallest man I had ever seen. He was an African with jet black skin and full lips. He was wrapped in a large multi-coloured robe. His head-dress consisted of a swathed dome-shaped turban of pure silk. He smiled, exposing gleaming white teeth.

It occurred to me that he would have many wives and would require a gift for each of them. I thereupon began to show him the European gifts, but he was not interested. Suddenly he spoke in a squeaky high-pitched voice. "Have you anything for a little baby?" he whispered.

Later I learned from the newspapers that he was the Lisa of Lagos, passing through Singapore *en route* to the Melbourne Olympic Games.

CHAPTER
TWENTY-THREE

Under the Curfew

At weekends we used to visit the palm-fringed swimming pool at Seletar Air Force Base or the Britannia Club Pool which was situated opposite Raffles Hotel. It included a ballroom, library, dining room and a games room and restaurant.

The Club was donated to the troops in the British Army by the late Lord Nuffield, the millionaire philanthropist who founded the Morris Cowley car firm in England. We also enjoyed trips to Johore, which was reached by crossing the causeway joining Singapore to Malaya. Here we visited the Sultan of Johore's Palace and a magnificent mosque which contained superb crystal chandeliers brought from Czechoslovakia.

Another visit was to the Johore Zoo which, we were told, was run by the illegitimate son of the Sultan of Pahang.

On our return from Johore we were faced with an ugly political situation. There had been a Communist-inspired uprising against the British people. Cars had been overturned with their occupants still inside them.

The next day seemed fairly quiet while I went about my work in the boutique so I decided to join my friends who were attending a dance at the Britannia Club that evening.

It was an enjoyable affair when, out of the blue, a voice came over the microphone. The voice stated that all service families were not permitted to leave the building as rioting was in progress outside and a curfew had been declared.

We carried on dancing and talked with our friends, one of whom was a young sailor hoping to see my daughter, but she had not arrived to join us. He had brought her a present from Hong Kong but I don't think that she was too keen on him.

Suddenly I turned round to see him gasping for breath and doubled up in pain. I remembered that he had only been drinking orange juice. A tall, fair young man carried him out into the entrance hall.

An ambulance was called but without results. We were told that all available ambulances were out picking up the rioters.

After some time, an officer decided to take him in his car to the British Military Hospital which was on the other side of town. There was nothing I could do but make a gangway through the already crowded foyer, help him into the car and accompany him to hospital.

We passed a convoy of armoured cars. Armed soldiers were placed strategically at sandbagged gun emplacements.

It was midnight when we arrived at the hospital. A body on a stretcher was being carried in. A doctor examined our sailor friend and pinpointed the trouble as stomach cramp, brought on by food poisoning, and it was decided that he be returned to sick bay on board his ship, HMS *Newcastle*.

By this time the sailor began to recover. He thanked me for helping him and summoned a taxi for me.

The driver, a Chinese, assured me in broken English that he liked British people and that I would be safe with him. However, halfway home we were flagged down at a police road block, and asked where I had been and what was my destination? The police then informed me that the curfew was on and I must go home and stay there or I could be shot.

Approaching our road, I noticed that barricades were everywhere and armed police patrolled the estate. The house was in darkness; my husband and children were fast asleep. In the morning newspapers there were reports of cars being overturned complete with occupants and burned during the night. On listening to the radio we were informed that Singapore was under curfew and there was a penalty of 500 dollars or one year in jail for anyone who ventured out into the streets.

An Army jeep arrived and we received a list of instructions. The next three days were spent confined to our homes, allowed out for only half an hour to buy groceries and bread. A helicopter hovered overhead giving out amplified messages and instructions.

According to radio news reports, rioters had caused havoc, overturning traffic lights, bus shelters and cars until the riot squads had rounded them up and confined them to jail.

Joe was not allowed to leave barracks at this time and we did not worry, knowing that, had worse things occurred, we would have been taken in armoured trucks to the safety of the General Military Headquarters.

CHAPTER
TWENTY-FOUR

A Variety of Events

After peace was restored, Joe became restless to resume his hobby of presenting classical recorded music programmes to the public, and he felt it was time to form a new organisation in Singapore. The question was — would it take on in an Asian country? If it did, it would be the first one in Singapore.

I suggested that he should write a letter to the *Straits Times*, a widely read newspaper, asking if anyone was interested.

The letter duly appeared in the paper and the replies were overwhelmingly in favour. A hall was soon found in a large educational institution. It was the Oui Tiong Ham Hall, better known as St Joseph's College for Boys, in Bras Basah Road.

Expensive sound equipment was donated by a Chinese millionaire. From then on Joe became steeped in his hobby of compiling and presenting a weekly recorded symphony concert to large and appreciative audiences. Not only were the Chinese and Malays appreciative, they were also exceedingly well mannered and co-operative. Other regular members of the audience were Army and Air Force personnel, including a

Brigadier and other officers from Pasir Panjang. One programme included the Thai Ambassador and members of his party.

In October the monsoon rains arrived — in torrential sheets and drenching the hot earth. The air was filled with steamy vapour. Our first Christmas soon caught up with us.

As the festive season approached we made the usual preparations and the same magic filled the air that we remembered back in England. The rains had stopped and Christmas night was clear, save for a few joss sticks burning in nearby Chinese homes.

On Christmas morning we were awake early. There was brilliant sunshine and a clear blue sky. The children were happy with the plastic Christmas tree and, of course, their presents.

We all went to Mass at Seletar Air Force base and came home to a light turkey lunch with ice cream to follow. After lunch we piled into the car for a trip to Changi Beach to laze and bathe in the cool water until darkness fell on the outline of the distant jungles across the Straits of Johore.

The next months I spent attending to the numerous American tourists who were visiting the boutique and helped prepare fashion shows to be held in the hotel ballroom.

Doris Geddes was also preparing for one of her numerous trips abroad, when Tina and I would be alone in the boutique to cope with all kinds of requests from tourists and other regular customers. One such instance concerned an Australian couple in their early forties, who were so obviously enraptured with one another that it was difficult to negotiate with them at all.

The lady had chosen a beautiful housegown of pale pink Chinese silk brocade. Whilst in the fitting rooms, the couple began to make wild, passionate love and nothing we said could separate them. Finally, the bill was presented, but even that could not quell the flames. It was my friend Tina who decided to call one of the porters from the hotel, who by his presence seemed to do the trick.

One day we received a phone call from the Sultan's Palace at Johore. The Sultana would be calling that day and a time was arranged. I remembered that Doris Geddes had designed her coronation gown, and it was featured on the front page of our printed brochure.

The lady — a very elegant Romanian by birth — arrived with her daughter Miriam, the English governess, the secretary, a detective, and last of all the syce, or chauffeur, who seated himself in the garden rather than wait in the large Rolls-Royce parked outside, with the family crest placed above the number plate.

Coffee and biscuits were served from the hotel while the Sultana chose expensive fabrics to be used in the making of her gowns in selected styles. Miriam was being corrected by the governess for stuffing biscuits into her mouth.

"Don't eat like a little piggy," said the governess.

"Mum, she is calling me a pig," came the quick retort.

I believe that Miriam is a very elegant lady today.

Another day we had a visit from a pretty young English girl in her early twenties. She was engaged to marry a Chinese young man and was accompanied by three elder Chinese women. Together they chose the most expensive French lace, in a creamy white. The day came for the first fitting, but all was not well. The English girl complained that Thin Tailor had flattened her beautiful and ample bust line. It was obvious that he was more at home with the slender figures of the Chinese women, although I tried tactfully to explain to him that a little more room was needed.

However, she explained to me that her fiancée's relatives were buying the dress and she had to abide by their wishes.

When she arrived for the final fitting I noticed that her face, arms and legs were spotted with daubs of blue gentian dye. She told me that the night before she had fallen into a monsoon drain and was covered in bruises.

The Chinese had used their own cure, which had badly stained her skin.

The wedding day arrived and she phoned to ask whether they could use the garden of the boutique for wedding photographs, to which we readily agreed. Her Chinese husband was a delightful, plump and jolly character and we concluded that all had gone well.

The famous American millionaires' ship was in Singapore, so it meant that I must stay late in the evening. I had already taken a taxi out to the ship in the morning to deliver our beautiful printed brochures to the tourists. Many of the rich Americans thought I was a Singapore guide and offered me large sums to show them around the town, but I was needed back at the boutique.

138

That evening we received a phone call from Philip Halsman, the photographer from *Time* and *Life* magazines. He wished to take photographs of our expensive silk gowns and stoles. He was having a beauty queen flown down from Malaya to model the gowns.

I rang Doris Geddes, who was now back from her holiday abroad. Yes! she agreed, and I was to supervise his visit. Tina had gone home, so that I was alone when they arrived about 9.30 p.m.

Silks of all colours were produced; vivid reds, shades of greens and blues, hand-loomed and interwoven with gold thread. Soon the garden was ablaze with arc lights and large cameras were set up on tripods. I watched the procedure with interest and was able to give advice as to the arrangement of the materials used.

It was 11 o'clock when they finished. I had been suitably reimbursed for working overtime and my husband was waiting patiently with the car to take me back to Serangoon.

It was my duty to call at the desk of the hotel foyer every morning and make a list of the new arrivals to the hotel. They would then have a printed brochure sent to their suites or rooms. Sometimes I would see an armed guard outside the suite of a high dignitary from some remote state. On one occasion Doris asked me to take a message to a Chinese man working at the desk in the foyer. I thought the man spoke insultingly, so I reprimanded him, but before I could reach the office he had followed me in a fit of rage. It seemed he had lost face in front of his colleagues. Doris asked me to soothe him down. I explained that I had not realised how

139

clumsy I had been in showing him up in front of his co-workers. I went back to make amends, as in a tropical climate tempers soon flare up and one could easily find a knife at the throat.

CHAPTER
TWENTY-FIVE

Chinese New Year

It was already February and from the sound of the exploding firecrackers we knew that Chinese New Year had arrived. It was the Year of the Cockerel and the celebrations continued with gusto for 15 days.

Forty-six years before Sun Yet San ushered in the Western Calendar, the following rites were used and are still used today. Each day had a special ceremony connected with some ancient custom.

Early on New Year's Day the head of the family opens the main door. This is known as opening the gate of wealth. Heaven and Earth are worshipped. A table spread with offerings is placed in the reception hall in front of a small statue of Buddha. The head of the family kneels three times, places incense in the censer, takes a paper horse, gives thanks for past favours, begs to be protected from sickness and prays for success in business. Then he sets fire to mock paper money and detonates fire crackers. The gods having been worshipped, the family now pay their respects to relatives. Adults are served hot tea and nibble tobacco and water melon seeds.

The second day is the birthday of dogs and the god of wealth is worshipped. The third day is the birthday of hogs, when mock money is offered to the god of wealth. The fourth day pertains to ducks, when bathing establishments are opened and religious rites practised. The fifth day is of oxen and the god of wealth of the five directions is worshipped. Fire sticks are ignited and mock money burned. Day six is of horses and the seventh day is the commemoration of the day on which man first appeared and thanks is given for existence. If there is sunshine on that day the whole year will be happy. The eighth day is the birthday of rice; the ninth, of vegetables, is also the birthday of the Pearly Emperor Yuah Sheng. If who is known as the Lord of the Physical World. On the tenth day, wheat and barley are honoured; on the eleventh, preparations are made for the festival of lanterns. The twelfth day is a day of rest. On the thirteenth day, lamps are placed on tombs. These are called ghost lamps, intended to guide the disembodied spirit back to the grave.

The fourteenth day is a day of rest and the fifteenth day is the day of the first moon in China. It is also the day on which the festival of lanterns takes place. There is much merriment and unmarried girls are let out to see the display of lanterns and watch the dragon dance.

Childless women endeavour to procure one of the candle ends. One is taken and laid on the bedspread in the hope that the woman will be blessed with children.

Today in Singapore the dragon is paraded through the streets, swaying this way and that, and people celebrate until the last firecracker has exploded and life, once again, returns to normal. There is never a dull moment in Singapore, as we soon found out.

The next festival was the celebration of Thaipusam, in which I was inadvertently caught up one morning on the way to work. I happened to be sitting on the front seat of a bus which was held up because of a long procession of Indians. It was the Hindu Festival of Penance, in which Hindus who have taken a vow to do penance for their past sins offer homage to the six-headed god of Hindu mythology — Lord Subramanyan.

The penitents carried wooden arches on their shoulders, called Kavadis, their bodies resembling human pincushions, with spikes of silver and steel buried into their flesh — on their chests and backs, and skewers piercing their cheeks and tongues. It is said that for a fortnight before this they deny themselves all luxuries.

The mythical story behind the festival of Thaipusam is that it was the day on which the god Subramanyan appeared before the world.

Siva's consort — Parvathi — was having her ablutions in a sacred tank in India when a lotus flower appeared on the water. As she gazed in wonderment at the mysterious flower, it evolved into a six-headed baby. The name of the god Subramanyan means "divine law giver".

I was told that the Hindus had walked from the Perumal Temple in Serangoon Road, and were on their way to the Chettiar's Temple in Tank Road where the deity was enshrined. Hundreds of tourists lined the street with cameras clicking. One devotee must have had 200 needles sticking in his flesh. Someone was pouring liquid into his mouth. He seemed to be in a trance-like state.

I arrived late at the boutique, but Tina was holding the fort.

Our next treat was far less frightening. We had heard that the Australian aircraft carrier *Melbourne* was in port, and as Kevin was now beginning to take an interest in ships and naval affairs, I thought it might help him decide on his future career.

I happened to have the day off from work, so we took the Singapore Contraption Company bus (the correct word is Contraction — but we thought it suited the bus better). As we passed down Serangoon Road we noticed a large sign: "The British Exterminating Company". A little further down was the Revivalist Society's head-quarters. After our bones had suffered a thorough jolting, we alighted at the quay, where a launch was waiting to take us to the aircraft carrier. The sea air was refreshing after the heat of the island and the slight aroma from the Singapore River — or "Stinkapore", as so aptly named by Bernard.

The sea was smooth as we left the shelter of the quay and made our way to the enormous hull standing high above the water. We climbed aboard.

Soon we were going up and down on the movable flight deck. We watched a plane rev-up and then, to the aggravation of a group of visitors, emit black smoke right in their faces.

Feeling thirsty, we were about to take some water from a nearby tap when a young officer came to our aid with cups of iced water from the mess. He then proceeded to show us around the aircraft carrier. We were so interested in all the details being explained by the young officer that suddenly Josephine and Roberta had worried looks on their faces. It seemed that we were the only visitors left on board and all the launches had left. Kevin and Bernard were enjoying themselves so much that we had lost all sense of time.

A voice behind us inquired, laughingly, "Are you staying the night?" It was an officer, who reassured us that the Captain's private launch would be at our disposal. Of course, our young daughters and the two boys were delighted.

CHAPTER
TWENTY-SIX

Our Friend Maria

We arrived back at the quay in style and the children had lots to talk about when their father returned home.

Joe had invited a famous Malay film star to present the next programme at his recorded symphony concert. He thought that a change of face, especially one as beautiful as Maria's, would capture a larger audience.

Maria had just finished making a Malay film under the sponsorship of the famous Shaw brothers, both Chinese millionaires. The venue was to be the YWCA on Beach Road. The concerts, as usual, were free of charge. A collection was made to cover the hire of the hall. The small amount of profit from the sale of refreshments was ploughed back into the Society for new records.

The concert was a great success and was attended by people of all nationalities, some having to stand at the back. The local Chinese businessmen were only too anxious to supply the best equipment free of charge for just a mention of their particular firm on the printed programme. Even the programmes were printed free by businesslike Chinese sponsors.

Maria seemed happy to present the programme and reciprocated by inviting us to her home for dinner at 7pm, a few days later.

146

The evening turned out to be one of the most eventful and pleasant of the three years we spent in Singapore. Not only did we enjoy the delicious meal that Maria had prepared for us with her own hands, but to the delight of the children we learned that her husband — Abdul Razak — was the manager of the large amusement park known as the "New World" which was unique in the whole of Asia for its variety of entertainments. After dinner we sat in the garden under the palm trees and sipped cool drinks until a fat, jolly Chinese man arrived. We were told by Abdul that he was Mr Siong, the cameraman, and was to join us on the trip into town. He took the four children in his car and Maria and Abdul came in our car.

It was a lovely evening, with the fragrance of frangipani everywhere, and the bay was a lovely sight with myriads of lights bobbing up and down on the rippling tide.

It was not long before the children were testing the dodgem cars, the ghost train and the ferris wheel; even I jumped on a large roundabout with Bernard, and as we slowed down I could hear laughter and saw Tina with her husband and two small children. We chatted for a while, then Mr Siong was anxious for us to see the Koon Tow Fighters, who were demonstrating their abilities in the art of fencing with parangs. These are long knives which are brandished to the accompaniment of rhythmic movements, the feet being kept wide apart.

Maria guided us to a dance floor to watch the modern jogget dancing, where Asian girls sit in rows or at tables surrounding the dance floor. Male partners buy tickets

147

from a desk, enabling them to dance with the girl of their choice.

The girls are dressed modestly in long sarongs or colourful kebayas, a type of blouse. They appear bored and dance at least half a metre away from their partner.

Bernard, Roberta, and Kevin were beginning to get sleepy after all the excitement and Mr Siong offered to take them home. It was nearly midnight when Maria and Abdul asked us whether we had seen the death houses of Sago Lane.

We drove from one New World to a completely different world of bright lights, garish colours, and noisy street cafés. This was where the Chinese sent their old people when they were about to die, the main reason being that their homes are so crowded that there isn't room for them.

The houses contain cubicles with rows of double bunk beds where the old people recline, waiting for the end, to the accompaniment of blaring music from the cafés, hammering from the coffin shops and the noise of the ever-passing crowd. One shop had a large wooden coffin. A young girl was kneeling beside it, clothed in sackcloth. There was a photograph of a woman of approximately 48 — perhaps the girl's mother!

Outside there was an altar to Buddha, where joss sticks were burning. Someone had made an offering of a bowl of rice and a bunch of bananas. The girl looked sadly into my eyes as I mourned with her for a few minutes.

Each shop had festoons of coloured paper articles — boats, houses, aeroplanes — that the passers-by bought to burn for the departed spirits. All night long the noise and flashing lights of the neon signs made a strange contrast to the silent bodies of those about to leave this world. We left the bizarre scene as Maria and Abdul had booked seats for us to go to the midnight showing of the film *Sayonara*. We were glad to rest in the modern and comfortable cinema. It was 3.30am when we took Maria and Abdul home and thanked them for a really delightful evening. They wanted us to stay for coffee but we needed to get home to the children.

Maria's participation in the Recorded Music Society was so popular that my husband asked other well-known people to present programmes. One was a famous radio announcer, another a city councillor, and several concerts were given for charitable purposes. The Cheshire Homes benefited by $500, as did a young girl who had to be sent to London for a throat operation.

On one occasion Joe had asked the Chief Minister to come along with his wife, to address the audience and say a few words of encouragement to the Society. We were delighted when Mr Lim Yew Hock, the Chief Minister of Singapore, and his wife accepted the invitation.

For this occasion we hired the hall of St Joseph's Boys' College, or the Oui Tiong Ham Hall, thanks to the kindness of the Brother Director. We were warned that as the Chief Minister had had a few threatening letters because of the political situation, there would be 50 armed policemen surrounding the building.

Roberta, now nine years of age, was waiting behind the stage with a large bouquet of orchids to present to

Mrs Lim. Roberta made her little speech of welcome which she had been rehearsing for some time. Mrs Lim leaned over and kissed her on the cheek. Mr Lim smiled and positioned her between them while press photographs were taken.

The couple stayed for the rest of the programme. Mr Lim sat next to the Brother Director of the college and I sat next to Mrs Lim.

This was the highlight of Joe's concerts. It gave him so much pleasure bringing the music of the masters to capacity audiences, although he did not make a cent of profit out of the programmes.

CHAPTER
TWENTY-SEVEN

Deep into Chinatown

One night, a friend — the wife of a soldier living on the estate — accompanied me for a walk into the Chinatown area of Singapore. We were to go in search of some curtain material. When we arrived, the shops were overflowing with bustling life. Old Chinese men and women crouched on their heels minding younger children. Bamboo poles displayed festoons of washing. Gangling youths slouched at shop corners. Some gathered in groups outside crumbling walls.

The shops were lit by neon lights and there was a pungent smell from charcoal fires where rice was being cooked. As we crossed the busy street, we saw a group of Asian men of all ages, seated cross-legged on a patch of grass under a shady tree. In front of them was a small table. It was the storyteller of Chinatown, who took his place at the table and began to capture the attention of the listening audience.

On making inquiries, I learned that he was speaking in Mandarin and that he was known as Uncle Ho. My informant told me that he had been telling stories in Chinatown for the past 28 years and had studied at the Fu Fan University of China. He had also taught in a

Singapore kindergarten, but had to give up his job because of tuberculosis, which he alleged was cured by smoking opium. Many Chinese were illiterate, so that their only news came from Uncle Ho. It appeared that Uncle Ho had been arrested for telling stories in Burma, Indonesia and Indo-China. Was he, perhaps, the well-known leader, Ho Chi Minh, that we read so much about in the Vietnam War, using this subtle approach to spread his doctrine of Communism? One would require a knowledge of Mandarin to understand the real meaning behind his tales. His thin face and goatee beard were not dissimilar from those of Ho Chi Minh.

As we passed deeper into the human jungle, a throbbing lifestyle of joy and pain, weakness and strength, we saw a Chinese man seated on a wooden chair placed on the sidewalk. He was screaming in pain while a quack Chinese dentist had one of his teeth firmly in his grip. A crowd of onlookers watched closely and were convulsed with laughter; some even clapped their hands.

The dentist used no drugs to deaden the pain of the extraction. His entire stock-in-trade was a rusty pair of forceps and a few bottles of red liquid. A small lump of clay was displayed, on which gleamed the neatly arranged teeth of his past customers.

I was told that these quacks acquired their knowledge from their forefathers, whose origin was lost in the mystery of Chinese history.

One long tug and the dentist triumphantly held the offending tooth aloft while the poor patient took flight in panic. The crowd cheered. The nearby juke-boxes blared out their jingling sounds and the next customer took the chair.

As we wended our way through the busy throng, an ambulance screamed to a halt outside a coffee shop. The rickety chairs and tables had been overturned and there was a pool of blood on the floor near the counter. My friend edged me away from the ghastly scene but, being curious, I was told that there had been a gang clash involving two secret society members and that there was a danger of acid being thrown.

My friend and I jumped in a taxi and made for home, having forgotten all about the curtain material. We related our experiences to our husbands, who were having a quiet drink on the patio, and they were horrified to learn that we had explored the "out of bounds" area which is forbidden even to the British troops. Little did we know that if we had been seen by the Military Police, we could have been sent back to England forthwith.

On reading the history of Chinese secret societies, I found that they were as old as Singapore itself.

Soon after Stamford Raffles arrived, the Chinese people became attracted to the tin mining in Malaya and began to leave their homeland and infiltrate into these areas. Then, seeing the importance of Singapore, they made the island their home, at the same time forming these Triad societies. They were originally intended as benevolent institutions, but degenerated later into criminal organisations and their strength grew as Singapore expanded and flourished.

Two hundred dollars was the sum paid to any member. On the death of that member the sum was paid to the next of kin. The societies, of which there are 365 (this number was correct when I was in Singapore in the years 1955-1958), had a membership of approximately 20,000 Chinese people. They had their "strong arm" sections or killer groups, the most notorious group being the Ang Bin Hoay, or Red Faced Triad Society made up of Hokien Chinese. Formerly known as the Hung Society, it derived its name from five monks who, in the Ming Dynasty, ran from a burning monastery which was set ablaze by the Manchus at Kho Khy in Kantung, South China. They were saved from the pursuing Manchu troops by five horse dealers and taken to a temple, where they met a priest known as Chan Kan Nam.

Chan was a high official of the Manchu Government, forced to give up his position because of his intrigues. Chan joined forces with the five monks and formed the Hung Society, with five divisions, each consisting of a major lodge and a minor lodge. The lodges still exist in the Ang Bin Hoay Society of Malaysia. The Wah Kee secret society is the next most powerful society in Malaysia. It is said to have originated in Singapore in 1856, set up by a leading member of the fourth lodge of the Hung Society who fled from South China after disagreements with members of the other lodge. There are numerous other gangs, such as the Butang Tima gang of Kedah, and the Axe or Kapak gang of Kelantan.

The methods used today, and since the menace began, are intimidation and protection rackets involving stallholders, prostitutes, shopkeepers and travelling wayang groups. The wayang is a troupe of Chinese travelling players. The method used is to offer protection from rival gangs on payment of a fixed weekly sum of money, accompanied by the threat of injury or even murder if the payment should not be forthcoming. The stallholder would rarely call the police for fear of terrible consequences befalling him or members of his family. It is only after a victim is found brutally stabbed to death that the police can attempt to make inquiries in order to trap the assailants. Great strides have been made to wipe out this cancer. Many gang members have been caught and severely punished.

One of the biggest blows since a police raid at the Ang Bin Hoay headquarters in Penang in 1946 was the mass arrest of 22 Ang Bin Hoay leaders in Kuala Lumpur in May 1953. All were banished to China. Among them there had been a government committee of six, including a secretary; these were duly banished with the others.

This committee had been instrumental in imposing the death penalty, corporal punishment and fines on erring members. They were also responsible for a member's promotion and had detailed reinforcements to send to other states in times of rioting. Their powers included assassination of government officials and others.

All classes of the community had been forced to join these criminal organisations and before long new members were signing up at the rate of 1,000 a week.

On taking recruits, most of the societies hold initiation ceremonies. The Ang Bin Hoay ceremonial is an elaborately gruesome spectacle, the various stages of the ceremony corresponding to incidents in the life of the founder of the society, including the adventures of the monks from the burning monastery, their southbound flight and final reunion. Then comes a long catechism, after which the middle fingers of the initiate are pricked with a needle, their blood is mixed with some wine and a solemn oath of fidelity and secrecy is taken at the time of drinking this fluid. A white cockerel is decapitated as a symbol of the fate which will overtake traitorous members. The meetings often take place in the jungle.

The Ang Bin Hoay was dissolved in 1946 following continuous police action. It culminated in a raid in which most of the members were caught and finally banished. The splinter groups spread out over the various provinces of Malaya.

Now, the societies go by numbers and not names, such as the 0.8 group and the 24 gang, and are identified by their accompanying tattoo marks on arms and bodies.

The war against the societies continued unabated.

The government of Singapore was doing all possible to be rid of this menace.

CHAPTER
TWENTY-EIGHT

A Strange Legend

When I arrived at the boutique I thought it would be interesting, but I was quite surprised to find that it was a little more interesting and exciting than I had expected.

From the sunlit door leading in from Bras Basah Road, a tall Indian was approaching, clothed in a white muslin loincloth. He was groaning and making loud grunting noises; he seemed to be in a state of trance, with eyes staring wildly ahead.

That did not particularly frighten me until he walked towards an American couple and their daughter who had just entered the boutique from the hotel doorway.

He stood behind the young girl, his hands around her neck but not touching, at the same time grunting loudly. We stood spellbound whilst he transferred his position to the lady, as if he were about to strangle her. I approached the husband and whispered, "My God — he's mad." He, the husband, as transfixed as I was, seemed afraid to move for fear that the man would produce a knife.

I then hastened towards the office, where I wanted to warn Tina to call the police, but when I placed my hand on the door handle, the Indian fixed me with a wild stare as if to say: "Do it if you dare." However, I warned Tina

157

and she came out to talk to him. Knowing more about her Asian counterparts, she spoke sharply to him and was able to pacify him until I called a steward from the hotel. This action seemed to bring him out of his trance.

He thereupon walked quietly around the shop, combed his hair whilst looking in a wall mirror and departed, much to our relief. We then closed the street door until we recovered from what could have been a nasty incident. Tina phoned the police, but I don't know whether they found him amid the passing crowd.

Shortly after the incident, Doris Geddes' secretary arrived. She was the wife of one of the puisne judges of Singapore. She told us that there had been a meeting to elect the new Chief Justice and that her husband was in line for the position. We all waited for the news with excitement, but when the final announcement came we heard that a Chinese judge had been chosen. It was a sign that Singapore was soon to have its own government and self-rule was imminent.

Although we were nearing the end of our three-year term in the Far East, I must not neglect to mention one of the Malay legends. Our friend Maria Menado took the leading part in a film of it, under the direction of the famous millionaire brothers Run Run Shaw and Run Mee Shaw.

The story of the film was most unusual, unlike any British or European legend. The part itself was horrifying for such a beautiful woman as Maria. It was the story of Pontianak, a very old Malay legend in which some Malays still believe implicitly.

Pontianak, they claim, originated from a woman who died in childbirth and was double-crossed by a wicked witch who had given her a bad charm. The witch then told the devil that the woman was the new mistress of the bad charm. The woman, not knowing the origin of the charm, continued to use it. In giving birth to the child, the devil claimed the lives of both mother and child. She was duly buried, but the earth refused to accept her body; thus she became the Pontianak known in the legend.

Maria told me that the Malay people love these gruesome stories.

In delving into other Malay legends, I found them to be all bound up fiercely with superstition, more so than in any other country. It is believed by the more illiterate Malays that should a woman die in childbirth, her fingernails should be inscribed with words from the Koran. Some believe that a Bomoh, or witch doctor, should be called in to say prayers which will drive away evil spirits.

It is said that Pontianak appears in two different forms, one frighteningly different from the other. Sometimes Pontianak appears as a distorted woman, her breasts being at the back of her body. When she flits through the night air, her long sharp nails extend before her streaming black hair and her flight causes an eerie wailing sound. On other occasions she appears as a very attractive woman who likes flirting with men. She waits on a lonely road and lures men with her charms, but in whatever form Pontianak appears there is always a cavity in the back of her head. It is said that if this cavity is closed, the Pontianak will transform herself into a living woman. Many Malay people still believe this story to be true.

There is a story of an elderly Malay man who, as a young man, returned late from a cinema show and found a beautiful woman in his room. At first, he thought his parents had a guest and had forgotten to tell him. He noticed that the woman had a strange smile and that her feet did not touch the ground. He knew at once that this was the Pontianak.

The woman asked him to get close to her. He told her to wait, then went to the kitchen and returned with a nail, placing it in his pocket. He took the nail and quickly closed the cavity in her head. Pontianak's cries were loud and forceful while she slowly transformed herself into a normal woman.

Years passed by; the woman became his wife and eventually bore him a child. After the birth she became young and beautiful, while the man, unfortunately, became thin and ill.

When the child of the marriage reached the age of seven years, she noticed a nail in her mother's head. The child was told to fetch her father from work, which she did. By the time the man arrived, the woman had transformed herself back into a Pontianak, who, legend tells us, is a horrific vampire. The only way in which a woman can scare her away is by exposing her body. Pontianak, who is sensitive of her lack of physical charms, will flee in embarrassment. A man, legend tells us, can chase away Pontianak by holding the head of a

Puya fish. This fish has a spike and is the best defence against Pontianak and other evil spirits.

This story seemed so incredible that I can only assume it was used by women to scare their sons from the evil ways of the bad woman. As it has rolled like a stone throughout the centuries, it has gathered strange distortions of fact, until today the meaning is hardly discernible. I learned from Maria the method used for giving her the facial distortions which, when used, completely transformed her beautiful features.

She told me that it took a make-up man four hours to recreate the ugliness of Pontianak, and nearly as long to remove it. It was so hot underneath the heavy make-up, she said, that only one scene of one and a half hours' duration could be shot at any one time. For her change into the hunchback cripple, Chomel — the Pontianak in yet another form — the make-up time was more than two hours, and to beat the oppressive heat of the day, shooting took place by night.

A make-up expert had been flown in from India to carry out the task of turning the lovely Malay film star into an ugly monster. In the make-up expert's bag of tricks were four long fangs, putty, spirit gum, hanks of hair, a three foot-long wad of plastic, artificial pigments and dyes. The nose is the most difficult part to shape as it curves and crooks, allowing room for the nostrils. Maria had appeared in three Pontianak films, the titles of them being *Denden Pontianak, The Revenge of Pontianak* and *The Curse of Pontianak.*

I thanked Maria for telling us about her films and wished her good luck in her career.

161

The time soon came for us to say farewell to our Singapore friends. Joe's three-year tour of duty was rapidly drawing to a close and we, regretfully, were preparing to leave this fascinating island in the sun. Three happy years had elapsed so quickly. There was Tina, whom I had grown to love for her sweetness and patience. There was Doris Geddes, Thin and Fat tailors, Maria and her husband, and Joe's many friends from the Recorded Music Society.

Our return to England was arranged by Army Headquarters, Far East Land Forces. Our aircraft was a Handley Page four-engined Hermes.

The day finally came for us to board the plane and it was as if Singapore wanted us back again.

The plane took off, but forty minutes later we were back at Singapore Airport.

The pilot had calmly announced while we were in flight that there was a "minor defect" and we would be flying over the sea to jettison part of our load of fuel before returning to Singapore.

When we landed there was a row of fire engines and ambulances present. We were later informed that there had been some difficulty with the braking system.

After a short delay we took off again, the route being via Bangkok, Karachi, Calcutta — where we stayed for one night — then Abadan and Brindisi. We finally touched down at Blackbushe Airport. Home at last.

One freezing winter in England . . . and then off to Australia . . . but that's another story!

PART THREE

Emigration to Australia

CHAPTER
TWENTY-NINE

On returning to England from Singapore, we experienced the coldest winter for many years. The waves froze for a mile out into the North Sea, and the wind was worse than a whetted knife. We decided to emigrate to Australia, taking with us Roberta and Bernard.

Josephine, our eldest, was working in a bank and about to become engaged to be married, so preferred not to come with us.

Kevin had just joined the Royal Navy, and was away from home for long periods at a time.

Joe had recently retired from the British Army, and was now working with a plastics firm.

We were living in a five-bedroomed house that I acquired with the money left to me in my mother's will. It was decided that we would sell the house and make a profit.

The house required exterior redecoration, so a firm of housepainters was called in. It was while they were on the job that Joe had one of his brainstorms.

I was preparing lunch when he arrived on the scene, and I mentioned that Josephine's fiancé was coming to lunch. His whole demeanour changed, and he asked me why I had not informed him before. I couldn't find an answer. It seemed ridiculous to make an issue about the situation. However, his face became red and blue alternately as his anger mounted. Unable to remain in the kitchen with a raving lunatic, I turned off the gas and went upstairs, but he picked up an axe and followed me.

I darted towards one of the rooms on the second floor, but he cornered me on the narrow staircase. I was unable to get down. He began using vile language.

I spoke to him firmly and tried to calm him down. "Drop the axe and we'll talk." That did not work, so I lunged past him, ran down the stairs into the hall, and out to the front gate. One of the workmen was washing his brushes.

"He's gone berserk with a chopper!" I yelled.

The workman laughed as I disappeared up the road, stifling the tears. I kept on walking — one, two, three, four, five miles — until I reached the far side of Manston Aerodrome and then on to Birchington. I passed fields gleaming with ripe corn, interspersed with blood-red poppies. A policeman gave me an odd look and I realised that I was wearing my slippers. There was a pound note in my raincoat pocket, so I dived into the nearest shoe shop and bought a cheap pair of canvas shoes. I sank into the chair exhausted and, when I recovered, retreated into the nearest café and relaxed with coffee and a sandwich. There was enough money left for a bus back to Margate, and a seat in the cinema. I forget the name of the film, but it helped to take my mind off the episode. When I returned home, all was quiet.

Next day, I asked the doctor if anything could be done for Joe, and was told to see a marriage guidance councillor. Nothing would induce Joe to go. It was suggested that I take up art.

The schizophrenia that plagued my husband was never believed by people outside the family. In fact he would tell friends what a wonderful wife he had.

We sold the house, made £1000 profit, and moved to a three-bedroomed house in Westbrook, a few miles away.

Letters were arriving from Kevin, in the Royal Navy. It seemed that he was seeing life in the raw. He said the men come in drunk, some are homosexuals, and if you don't wash you get scrubbed with scouring powder. I regretted that I had let him leave home at such an early age. I wrote a letter to the Admiralty, and was told that it would be looked into. Seeing him on his first leave, he assured me that he was fit and healthy.

Emigration papers had been filled in and now the Westbrook house was put up for sale. There was one enormous problem — our English Retriever dog, Kim, who we loved as one of the family. We agreed that we couldn't leave him behind. We made inquiries as to how he could be shipped to Australia. A medical check-up was required, and papers signed by a Justice of the Peace. We required a kennel and a month's supply of dog food. All these plans were left in my hands as Joe was busy with his job at the plastics factory. He was sceptical about the duration of the job, and there was little industry in Margate, where we lived.

In due course we were offered a passage on the Sitmar line's ship, *Fairstar*. We had not sold the house, so we refused on those grounds. A month later we were offered a passage on the *Fairsky,* but still the house was unsold. We waited another month and were offered the P&O

167

ship *Canberra*. We sold the house at a lower price and accepted the invitation.

Before we vacated the house, for a temporary furnished flat, Josephine had announced her wedding day, so there was just time for me to design and make her wedding gown, and plan a reception. The wedding took place at our parish church and was a happy occasion.

The next hurdle was to despatch the dog. We took him on the train to the London docks, with his passport intact, and watched as he was hauled aboard the cargo ship. It was a very sad occasion and I think we all shed a tear.

We managed to sell our furniture and pack the rest of our belongings in large wooden crates.

Josephine had promised to look after Kevin on his home leaves, and we hoped that he would join us one day.

On the day of travel we were up early. I packed five suitcases ready to take with us. We left the furnished flat, took a taxi to Margate station and waited for the London Victoria train. Our destination was Victoria, Australia.

When we arrived in London, we took a taxi to Waterloo station, for the train to Southampton. On extracting our luggage from the taxi, we counted three cases. The other two were still standing at the taxi rank at Victoria. Joe jumped back into the taxi while I prayed, and thank God, he found the missing luggage still in position.

After leaving London in that late November of 1963, we said goodbye to the lovely English countryside. We kept our thoughts to ourselves, and yet we felt excitement for the new experience opening in front of us.

On arrival at Southampton, the white hull of the Canberra loomed in front of us. Josephine, her husband Michael, and Kevin, in his Naval uniform, were there to see us off. As the ship glided out of the quay, their figures became smaller and smaller. Dinner was being served, and a relaxed evening ensued. Joe joined the activities committee, while I took up reading, writing and making new friends.

The voyage took us to Naples, through the Mediterranean and the Suez Canal, down to Bombay and Colombo. Joe seemed to make his own friends; I only saw him when he came to the cabin at night. The children had fun crossing the line and received their certificates to prove it. Bernard wore a perpetual smile, and Roberta was now an attractive redheaded teenager. She made many friends, and received most of the attention from the good-looking waiter at the dining table.

The table was set for eight people, including a young couple from Lancashire, and a couple from east London, Bernard having his meals with the children.

It was obvious that the Lancashire couple were not used to the grand life. The menu, being printed in French, always sent them into a state of confusion, and when the waiter enquired if they would like "poisson", the wife declared in a strong Lancashire accent, "New, ah down's want no poison. Just give us fish and chips."

Another time, I was just about to take a mouthful of

soup when the lady from London blurted out, "Oi give the biby some orange juice, and it went roight through him," and then repeated, "roight through him." The Lancashire lass made good use of our delightful waiter, summoning him as often as possible for the slightest thing.

I was afraid to talk to Joe at table, as he always wanted to start an argument and draw people's attention, so I decided to say as little as possible. It would have been embarrassing if he had gone berserk in front of all those people. However, he seemed to be benefiting from the rest and the sea air, after his years of post-war struggle. I remembered what the psychiatrist had told me at Millbank Hospital in London — that if he had the slightest worry, he would take it out on the nearest person to him. Having an outgoing personality, he made friends easily, but somewhere inside there was a volcano waiting to erupt.

Our first glimpse of Australia came when we arrived at Fremantle. I took Roberta ashore with me, as Bernard had developed tonsillitis and Joe had volunteered to stay and look after him.

Roberta and I were very much impressed by the smartness of the ladies of Perth, nearly all wearing hats and cool summer frocks. The newly built quay and escalators were welcoming. The sandy soil and profusion of flowering hibiscus and other colourful plants, under a blue sunny sky, gave us a feeling of contentment. On viewing the Swan River, as we approached Perth, we were aware of being on the perimeter of a vast and beautiful country. We passed houses surrounded by palm trees, ferns and green lawns.

Roberta, now a teenage beauty, remarked on the good looks of the young men, and we started to sing "Where have all the young men gone?" We decided it was Perth. On reaching King's Park, we saw an enormous tree trunk, a kind of memorial to the large karri trees of the forests south of Albany. When we returned to the ship, Bernard had seen the doctor and was a little better.

We still had to encompass the Bass Strait, a very rough part of the Southern Ocean, and then sail into the Heads at Port Phillip Bay, before arriving in Melbourne. At the Heads, or Rip as it is known, there is a narrow strip of water, where a pilot is taken aboard to guide the ship through the swirling water, with sharp rocks on either side.

It was early morning when we arrived in Melbourne. We were all up on deck early to see the view and, after breakfast, join the queue for inspection of medical cards, immunisation papers and passports. Soon there was a mêlée of people, from all denominations, who had come aboard to offer their advice to migrants. We were not sponsored, so Joe asked for advice on accommodation. He was given the address of an expensive hotel, which, of course, was out of the question. It was only because of Bernard's condition that we were allotted a hostel. That being settled, we stood on the deck surveying the vast territory of Victoria. Every migrant must wonder what lies beyond. We said goodbye to our shipboard friends and went ashore to find our luggage in the customs hall. Two officials approached us, wearing grey twill coats. I wondered what was in their minds as they dealt with this Pommy family. One of the men searched through the layers of shoes, dresses and underwear. He extracted a shoe.

"Where have you been walking with this shoe?" he inquired, with an air of authority.

I looked at the offending shoe. It did have a small piece of grit embedded in the groove of the sole. "I wore it in England," I replied gingerly.

"Was it on a farm?"

"No!" I said, hoping that would settle the question, but he persisted.

"Was it in the country?"

Yes, but what had that to do with it?

"See these wooden beams holding up the customs shed?" he declared.

"Yes." I looked towards the painted posts.

"If one minute insect crept into those beams, the whole customs shed could collapse."

Strewth! But what had that to do with my shoe? We all looked puzzled. Was the man being over-zealous? I was afraid to utter one word, in case we would be clapped into jail. Who could argue with an Aussie in the course of his duty?

"I am afraid I will have to take the suitcase away for fumigation."

"How long will you keep it," I inquired nervously.

"About a fortnight," he replied.

"But those are all the clothes I possess."

At this stage, Joe fumbled for his cigarettes and passed him one. He accepted, and without another murmur he closed the case, chalked the OK sign on the side, and turned to the next customer. We breathed a sigh of relief, and were directed to a waiting coach.

Our accommodation consisted of a hostel in the vicinity of Jordonville, so that was where the coach was heading. Our driver, a cheery chap, wished us good luck and said he admired our courage. The evening was closing in as we arrived at a shanty town of Army sheds, with one large corrugated iron building that served as a canteen, with adjoining offices.

We queued up for a meal of mincemeat, pumpkin and peas. Afterwards we were given a key and shown to our hut. The hut was divided into three rooms, with beds for each of us and a pile of blankets and sheets. A list showing meal times was pinned on the door. The toilet and shower facilities were about three blocks away, and around a corner.

Next morning we woke early. People were walking about in their dressing gowns, towels and toilet bags slung over their arms. We soon learned the ropes. The showers were warm, but the cubicles were draughty and never properly cleaned. A large German woman would come daily with a hose and spray water on them, so that there were always puddles everywhere.

Roberta was already spoilt by the luxury of the *Canberra*. This was a new experience for her. I had learned to take the rough with the smooth, so that the shock was not so great for me. We made the Army hut as comfortable as possible, and took our place in the queue for meals. Joe always had a joke with the women serving masses of potatoes, greens, pumpkin and sausages. He always asked for kippers and custard, until one day he actually got what he asked for. He never asked again for kippers and custard.

As usual, the washing piled up, and I was conducted to the communal wash house, where there were deep, grey, concrete troughs with hot and cold water taps. There were some washing machines and a clothes line outside on the lawn. I soon found that the wash house was the camp nerve centre, where one learned all the latest scandal.

"How long have you been here, dear?" inquired a large lady with a small child tugging at her skirt.

"Two days," I replied.

"Wait till you've been here two years," she said pessimistically, and then gave me a run-down of all the people who had lived in the camp, bought cars and furniture, and then gone back to England.

While the women were doing the washing, one of the husbands was playing around with the children. Apparently, they were chasing each other with a bucket of water. I just happened to walk past a doorway and was the recipient of a full bucket of water, thrown in my face from an irresponsible parent, hiding behind a door. There was no apology, just a stupid grin.

It was the right time of the year to be in Melbourne, and there was so much to learn. A short train journey, and we were in the city, which is famous for its gardens and wide streets with tall trees on either side. The River Yarra was a quiet oasis for the business people working nearby.

Before we had time to feel homesick at seeing Christmas trees and fairy lights outside the one-storey houses, a message came from a nearby home in Jordonville. We were invited to spend Christmas day with their family. Apparently, a favourite aunt of mine, who lived in England, remembered that one of the sisters had a brother who lived in Jordonville. This was a release from our concentration camp-type of existence, and we were most grateful to be with this wonderful family.

After Christmas, we began to think about the sort of work we should do, and having attained that, the sort of house we should buy. We soon discovered that in January and February, in Melbourne everything closes. Nearly all the solicitors and estate agents are off on their summer holidays. Most factories close down; in fact it almost seems as if Melbourne comes to a standstill. Bernard was a constant visitor to our new friends" house.

Joe managed to get a job at a large car firm, as the plastics factory was closed. Roberta took a job at a large retail store. We all laughed when she came home and told us that they had placed her in the jewellery department, and a man had rushed in and hastily inquired, "Where's Manchester?"

"In England," came her bright reply. The "Manchester" was the name for the cotton and linen department.

I acquired a job in the exclusive dress department of a large store in the city. Things were very quiet, owing to the holiday season. The temperature had soared to 104F degrees, and I was supposed to stand all day long, trying to look busy, while waiting for a likely customer, but the few who came only wanted the "Ladies' Lounge". I found the standing tiring in the heat, so I sat down on the nearest chair and must have fallen asleep. Luckily, another inquiry for the Ladies' Lounge woke me up. Getting up at 6am on a scorching Melbourne day took some getting used to.

I had several jobs before I really settled down. One was at an exclusive gown shop in the fashionable Collins Street, where I could exercise my skill with the needle, and mix with pleasant company.

We bought a small car and put a deposit on a three-bedroomed, brick veneer house, only half an hour's train journey from Melbourne. A message came from the quarantine department to say that our dog had arrived and was in kennels on the other side of Melbourne. It gave the visiting hours. At the first opportunity, we piled in the car to visit our beloved animal. I don't know who was more excited, the dog or the family. Two more Sundays and we were allowed to take him home.

Bernard went to the local Catholic school until he was ready for the technical school.

During the next few years we all worked extremely hard, as well as establishing our new home. We sometimes visited the mountains or the beaches at weekends. Joe found an all-night job, so he had to have a room of his own in which to sleep during the day. When he awoke, he would have a meal and listen to his symphony music on the stereogram. He liked to be alone and to play the music as loud as possible. After a day at work in the city, I would return on the train, walk a mile to our home, and cook a meal for the family. After dinner there would be some tidying up to do, or more sewing. I would be lying if I pretended that all was well with our marriage. The shouting increased, the knife threats, and the act of pushing me across the room. I suppose the doctor would say it was due to a multitude of things; stress at work, being over committed with hire purchase bills. Joe seemed unable to keep a job for longer than a few months. There was always someone at work that he could not get along with. Strangely, he never had any difficulty finding another job.

Joe always insisted on doing the Saturday shopping in the supermarket. His list contained things that I would not have bought. There were several packets of chocolate biscuits, cartons of cigarettes and large jars of peanuts, a joint of meat, sausages and the same vegetables week after week. I often implored him to let me do the shopping, as there were so many small things that I needed, such as stock cubes, herbs and dried fruit.

Every week I gave him some of my earnings towards the food. I provided Bernard with school clothing and school books. Joe had chosen the furniture, television, washing machine and beds at a cheap hire-purchase firm in Melbourne, without my approval. When I protested, he had another brainstorm. My argument was proven when my bed collapsed in the middle of the night, although my weight was normal for my age.

Joe's bad tempers were becoming more frequent, especially at weekends, when he became like a madman, using obscene language and directing his hatred at me. The only thing for me to do was to go out for the day, knowing that when I returned he would be back to normal.

To get to the nearest beach took me at least one hour. First I had to take a train and then a bus. I could then walk along the beach, wearing a pair of dark glasses to hide my eyes, red and swollen from crying. It was a relief to breathe the fresh sea air.

There were several incidents after this, such as when Joe forced a lighted cigarette down my cleavage. I still have the scar today. The skin was burned on both sides of the breast, and I had to receive medical treatment. The doctor informed me that if Joe disfigured me again, he would be in danger of being committed to a mental home.

The next occasion occurred when I was seated in a lounge-chair at the side of the house, reading a book. I had been cleaning the windows of the house, outside and inside, and was exhausted. Joe got in the car and drove it towards me, braking suddenly as he reached the chair. I jumped up in fright and he laughed loudly.

I was very distraught by this time, trying to cope with the effects of the change of life, the hot flushes and frequent outbursts of tears, and worrying about the effects on the children. I began to feel like something the cat dragged in.

Here again, my faith in God was my greatest help. I remember one night almost crying out loud, "Almighty Father in Heaven, please send someone to love me. Someone who can see some good in me."

Next day, I looked in the mirror at my eyes, swollen with tears, and I said to myself, there and then, "Every time you cry, you disfigure the face that God gave you."

My hair was still naturally wavy, had turned from

red-gold to a warm blonde. The English air had given me a good complexion. My brown eyes were my best feature. My figure was, shall we say rounded? A little less chocolate and it could almost be back to normal. I always used a little make-up, not enough to look conspicuous. In fact, I came to the conclusion that I still had quite a lot going for me.

I made up my mind that I would not cry again. My self-hypnosis seemed to work, and every time the knife came near my throat, or the abuse was unbearable, I kept saying to myself, "Your face. Your face. Remember your face. No one will look at you if you cry again."

After a day's work doing dress fittings at the back of the shop, in not too congenial conditions, I was expected to carry out expert work. When waiting for a train home I would invariably find them so crowded that it was standing room only.

My journey home meant a short walk to the station, where I waited at the same place on the platform for the red rattler, a rickety, 100-year-old train which had long passed its heyday. A kindly German gentleman always offered me his seat. At first I knew him as the man in the velvet jacket and the bow tie. We struck up a friendship and had many interesting conversations. I began to look forward to the red rattler. To me, it became the Orient Express. Every morning he was there, in the same carriage, and in the evening I was always sure of a seat. He was a little older than me, taller, with a merry round face, and laughter lines spread out from his eyes. We would discuss so many topics that the 30-minute journey became five minutes.

Some summer evenings the trains were unbearably hot, when the temperature soared to 104 degrees F. There was no air-conditioning, and we could hardly breathe. On one occasion there was another German seated the other side of me. I happened to have a fan in my handbag, so I fanned the three of us. Hans was beginning to teach me a little German, so I bought a book optimistically named *German in Ten Days*. I thought I would show off my knowledge, so I blurted out in German, "I am so hot." The Germans burst into fits of laughter. They explained that I had said, "I am hot stuff."

One evening I entered the carriage, the second from the end, and looked around, but all I saw was the tired, blank faces of the crowd, their heads hidden behind their evening newspapers. I felt my face drain of life. I knew that it showed. I walked home that evening feeling that the bottom had dropped out of my life. As I walked in the door, Roberta greeted me and I burst into tears.

"What's up, Mum? Are you ill?" she inquired.

"He wasn't on the train," I blubbered.

"You must be in love," she said, in her girlish wisdom.

I dried my tears, remembering my vow not to ruin my face, and prepared to cook dinner for the family. I am glad to say that Hans was on the morning train. He had been detained at work, and life was rosy again.

CHAPTER THIRTY

Roberta

Roberta, the brightest star and the apple of Dad's eye, was, and still is, attractive and intelligent. She still shared the family bronze hair and English complexion and possessed a slim figure.

I was thrilled when she told me that she would be on a television programme, and had also entered a competition to be held at the Melbourne Town Hall. For several years she had been having her voice trained. I was delighted when she won a silver cup for the best singing voice. She had worked very hard at a well-known store. Suddenly she decided that she wanted to go to England to see her sister Josephine, now happily married and with a newly adopted son. The holiday was a happy one. She enjoyed several weeks in England, but it was soon time to return home to Australia. The plane was booked for a Monday. On the Sunday prior to the flight, she was present at Mass in a nearby church in England. She suddenly turned to Josephine, white with fear, and said, "Something terrible will happen to the plane."

Josephine's retort was, "Nonsense. You are suffering from nerves."

Little did she know then that the wing of the plane would catch fire, after having left Heathrow. Roberta was asked by the air hostess if she would change places with a family who wanted to be together. That family were together in death.

The fire swept through part of the cabin and Roberta escaped with many others down the chute. Josephine and her husband were there to comfort her. Josephine told me afterwards that she slept with her that night to stop her from trembling. With great courage, Roberta took the next plane home, on the following day.

I received a 5am call from Melbourne airport. "Your daughter is safe," they said calmly, and I thanked God. When she touched down in Melbourne, there were many reporters from television and the newspapers to find out the full story. She lost all her luggage, but she was safe home.

The train conversations still continued, and I seemed to wear a perpetual smile and often felt as if I was floating on cloud nine. Joe's temper did not improve and there were times when he was out of work for long periods. The debts were mounting, and the mortgage was unpaid. Worst of all, Joe refused to discuss his problems with me. I was shocked to learn that he had taken out a second and third mortgage. At one period, it looked as if we would lose the house.

One busy Saturday morning, I was tidying up the house when the front door bell rang. Roberta answered it. It was Hans, who had brought us a present of a dozen fresh farm eggs. Roberta invited him in, and he met Joe and Bernard for the first time.

Joe was listening to some music by Tchaikovsky. A short conversation ensued, in which, to Hans' amusement, Joe called me Mrs instead of using my Christian name. I made some fresh coffee for all of us. I wondered what reaction Joe would have to this visit, but it was completely without emotion or comment of any kind. I had already told Joe about my meeting Hans on the train. Just a platonic friendship, I told myself.

Roberta had changed her job and was now working for a stockbroker in the city. She had several boyfriends about this time. This particular Saturday night she was invited out to a dance at a nearby town hall. I had already gone to bed when I was awakened by a man's footsteps coming up the pathway. I hastily put on my dressing gown and opened the door. It was a policeman.

"Your daughter," he said, "has been involved in a car accident. She was thrown out onto the roadside. She is all right."

We were both very shocked, but relieved that she had not lost her life. Next day, we went to visit her at the hospital, and learned that she had a broken arm, a broken leg, and her lovely face was sore where splinters of glass had penetrated. In spite of all that, she managed to force a smile. Apparently a car with two drunken men in it had swerved into them as they drove home from the dance.

We visited her every day until the day she came home, walking slowly with a stick. Her youthful bones soon healed. Her face showed no signs of the glass splinters. When you are a mother, you pray constantly for your children. I know that without those prayers it might have been a different story.

As soon as my daughter had fully recovered and was able to go back to work, it seemed a good opportunity for me to take a trip to England to see my other beautiful daughter. At the same time it would help me to stifle my feelings for Hans.

"Thou shalt not covet thy neighbour's wife," I kept telling myself. His wife had gone back to Germany and had stayed there a year. I suppose he was as lonely as I was, even with a husband. Many times Joe had screamed at me to "Get out", etc, etc.

I booked myself onto a Greek ship, packed my bags and was off. At least it would be a chance for the family to learn how to cope without me being there.

The first night at sea, I began to feel at home. The rocking of the ship sent me to sleep. Being waited on at table was a new delight. I was thrilled at the prospect of sailing through the Panama Canal and spending one whole day and night in New York. I danced every night, played deck tennis every day. I couldn't believe that one could enjoy life so much. While we were crossing the Atlantic I did a silly thing. I played deck tennis when the deck was slightly wet, slipped and fell heavily on my left arm. After consulting the ship's surgeon and having an x-ray, it was discovered that I had a two-inch crack in my upper arm bone. It was immediately strapped to my body and I was given tablets for the pain.

Soon the outline of the Scilly Isles came into view, and the coast of Cornwall. This was my first visit home to my beloved England, and I was determined not to miss the first glimpse of it.

The sea was unusually calm as we sailed into Southampton Water. When we arrived at the dockside, I stood at the gangway, surrounded by my baggage, still in some pain from my arm, and chatting to a German lady I had met on the voyage. Two of my male sports partners approached and each in turn planted a kiss of farewell on my cheek. The German lady was so surprised, she exclaimed loudly in German, "Vas is das!" I think she thought that there would be more to follow.

My daughter, her husband and newly adopted son were soon on the scene. We fell into each other's arms. Michael, her husband, placed the luggage in the car. We were soon driving through the English countryside to their home on the outskirts of London.

The house was set in a neat tree-lined street. I was to share a room with my new grandson, a beautiful baby with red-gold hair.

I slept well that night, but when I awoke, I could feel the throbbing pain in my arm. I looked towards the cot. Two little blue eyes were staring at me, and then, to make a closer scrutiny, the small figure rose and peered over the edge of the cot. Without a sound he just gazed at me. I said "Hello" quietly, expecting him to cry, but no sound came. For the first time in my life, I had met the cryless baby. Soon his mother came in to change his nappy, and I began to dress myself with difficulty.

When I joined my daughter for breakfast, she seemed edgy. It was seven long years since I had seen her. Adopting a baby was a new experience for her, for which she seemed completely capable. I told her about the wonderful trip I had enjoyed on the Greek ship.

"Oh, by the way, Mum, there's a letter for you."

It was from my platonic friend, Hans. "Please do not stay too long in England. I want you to come back soon," he wrote.

I told my daughter about the meeting on the train, and read her the letter, as there was nothing in it to shock her, although quite possibly she had heard the full story from Roberta.

Josephine's husband insisted that I have my arm examined by the local hospital. He took me in the car to the hospital, and waited while I had x-rays and the arm was strapped to my body.

Not satisfied with having a wash down every day, I decided to try and take a bath, without disturbing the bandages. I partly filled the bath and stepped in to enjoy the warm soapy water, but when I tried to get out, I was stuck. Luckily I hadn't locked the door. I yelled out to Josephine, and she quickly came and threw a towel over me, and gradually hauled me out. If she had been out shopping, I would have been in a real predicament. She still laughs about the time Mum got stuck in the bath.

Most of my friends lived in the vicinity of Margate, Kent. I rang a couple whom I had met just after the war. We lived in the same street, and had brought up our children together.

The greeting that I received was warm and welcoming. I was entreated to come straight away, and given instructions on how to find their new home.

I bought a ticket, gathered my luggage about me with my good arm, and boarded the next train to Margate. When I had settled down, my thoughts wandered to my oldest and very best friend who also lived in that area. She was then 80 years of age, and a very sprightly and active lady. She had nursed my grandmother in 1940. I had lost touch with her, then by a chance meeting I met her at Mass one Sunday. She was a very interesting person. As a trained nurse she had worked in the homes of film stars in America; in London many famous people owe their first few months of existence to this fragile, caring Irish lady.

Not only did she nurse the famous, but many years ago when working as a district nurse, and receiving a call from some gypsies living on the outskirts of London, on a stormy night she would trudge to some caravans parked in a distant field, attend at the birth of a baby, or give help to the dying. No money was ever taken for these services, for the simple reason that there was none available.

She never became rich, and now lived on an old age pension in a block of commission (council) flats.

As soon as she heard that I was in the area, she rang me and insisted that I spend a week with her at Cliftonville.

The visit was all arranged. It was just a matter of transferring from one good friend to another. As soon as I walked in the door, I felt at home.

She insisted that I visit other friends or go down to the beach as I wished. She would not take any monetary reward, so I provided as much food as she would allow me to bring to the flat.

I was also invited to visit another friend, who lived in a large house quite nearby. This very lovely Swiss lady was comfortably off and owned a beautiful house in a large garden, and to guard it, a magnificent white Pyrenean mountain dog.

She may have owed her life to the dog when two rather tough looking men called to say they had come to inspect the house. They pushed past her at the front door. The dog, sensing danger, bit one of the men on the hand. They left rapidly.

A week was spent with this charming person, and her two sons came to visit her.

My next sojourn was to Bournemouth, to visit a very old friend of my parents' family. Although she was suffering much pain in the legs, she showed great kindness and hospitality, and insisted on taking me on various coach tours to the New Forest and other interesting beauty spots.

I knew that my son's ship had returned to Portsmouth, which is not far from Bournemouth. I rang the dockyard. Yes, the ship was there and they would put me through to my son, Kevin. Unfortunately, he was out.

I had not seen him for seven years and he had been away at sea for 11 months. I was excited at the prospect of hearing his voice. They said they would ask him to ring me as soon as he returned.

My friend and I took it in turns to listen for the phone to ring. The phone remained silent. I then sent a telegram to the ship. No reply.

I had booked my passage back to Australia early that September, and had promised to visit a very dear aunt, who was a nun and lived at a convent in Hertfordshire, prior to my departure. Finally, in desperation, I rang the

Naval padre. On hearing of my sadness at not seeing my son, he declared that he would make it an order that my son visit me.

I thanked my friend for her kindness to me and continued on to the convent, where my aunt and all the Sisters gave me a very warm welcome. Whilst there, I received a phone call from my son to say he was on the way.

I was so excited that the nuns let me answer the door when he arrived. We kissed each other. He looked neatly dressed in a dark lounge suit. My aunt took us on a tour of the beautiful garden, where we talked happily. The Mother Superior had invited us to stay the night in the guest house, which was usually reserved for visiting bishops or priests. Kevin told me that he had applied for a job and was starting work the next morning. My aunt and I walked up to the station with him, said our goodbyes, and I remained to stay the night.

I felt a sense of relief that I had seen Kevin, but nonetheless I was still strangely puzzled.

Next morning I said farewell to the Sisters, who had been kindness itself to us both.

I took the train to London, where Josephine and her husband and baby son had come to see me off on the train to Southampton, where the *Achille Lauro* of the Lloyd Triestino Line was waiting for me.

The voyage back to Australia went very smoothly, apart from a cyclone that struck us in the Indian Ocean. There were the usual parties, Hawaiian nights, Neapolitan nights, fancy dress nights, and everyone was in a gay, romantic mood.

On one occasion I happened to be standing near the purser's office when I saw smoke coming from under a cabin door. I simply turned to the purser and said, "Excuse me, but I think the ship is on fire." Without a word, he grabbed the phone, and before I could turn around firemen had sprung from everywhere. It appeared that someone had left an iron on the board in the ironing room.

I shared a cabin with three very nice English ladies. One of the ladies, a spinster well into her sixties, had fallen head over heels in love with the Italian headwaiter, a dark swarthy man, quite a few years younger than herself. Sometimes when I had retired early for the night, he would come to the cabin, sit on her bunk and hold her hand. I wished that he would hurry up and go away, but if he saw that I was awake he would try and chat me up as well.

One night our very respectable 60-year-old was missing. We all began to worry when by early morning she had not returned to her bunk. At 4am the door opened, and in walked a very bedraggled, white-haired lady. Her clothes were rumpled and she collapsed exhausted on the bed. We were all anxious to know what had happened. This Romeo headwaiter had invited her to his cabin, which was somewhere down in the bowels of the ship. Her story was that he locked her in, and said that he would be back shortly. He didn't return, but another man came in to change his clothes. She was afraid to scream. When she managed to get out, she had to find her way back through a maze of passages, past bunks of sleeping crewmen, falling over as she negotiated steep iron ladders, until the cold light of dawn saw her a lone figure searching for her cabin.

When the cyclone blew up, the ship was tossed like a paper boat on a swirling torrent. It just happened to be my turn to visit the control room. I noticed a light that kept flashing red, so I inquired what was the reason for it and was calmly told that there was a fault in the ship that could not be repaired until we had come out of the cyclone.

We were soon sailing down the coast of Western Australia, making for Fremantle, where we had one whole day ashore. Then we sailed around the southern coast of Australia into the Bass Straits, before entering the narrow rip that leads into Port Phillip Bay.

On arrival in Melbourne, I was astounded to see my German friend standing on the quay waiting to greet me. We smiled and waved to one another. He indicated that he was happy to see me but that he had to return to his office. I felt happy that he had cared enough to come.

When the formalities were over, and I walked down the gangplank, there was no sign of my family, so I proceeded to get my baggage through the customs. There was nothing to declare, although I did get a suspicious look from the customs man when he extracted a large bottle of water with "Holy Water" written on the label. It was a bottle of water from the Grotto at Lourdes, that my aunt had given me.

Once in the crowded reception hall, I found Joe with Roberta and Bernard. It was lovely to see them all again and find out how they had managed in my absence.

The car was waiting to take me home.

CHAPTER
THIRTY-ONE

When Joe told me that he had some news for me, I knew that it would be bad news. He never seemed to have good news.

"I've lost my job," he declared. "I can't pay the mortgage. The water is going to be cut off, as I haven't paid the bill, and the hire purchase men are coming to take the television set away, as well as the washing machine."

The thing that worried me most was having to do the washing with just a trickle of water coming from the tap.

I somehow knew that it wouldn't be long before Joe found another job. He had the gift of the gab and, as my mother used to say, he could wheedle the heart out of a cabbage.

I wasn't looking forward to going back to my old job in the dark and cramped back room of a shop, especially as I had worked in the West End of London making gowns for royalty.

I began to scan the newspapers for some suitable rooms where I could work privately. It wasn't long before I found exactly want I wanted, and at a very low rent. It consisted of one long room, when I divided into two by adding a wardrobe complete with mirrors. I added two large mirrors, making a fitting room on one side of the wardrobe, and on the other side, by the window, was my workroom, complete with table sewing machine and ironing board.

The next step was to have some cards printed. I could only afford about 200 at first.

The room was on the first floor in a select area, so I had a sign made to place outside the front door. The sign was a deep blue colour with gold lettering, denoting that I was a London dressmaker and specialised in dress alterations only.

The train journey from home took a little longer than before but I did not mind, as my dear friend Hans was there to keep me company.

My premises were in the most fashionable area, just south of the River Yarra in a street lined with dress shops and other fashionable commodities.

Before the opening day, I spent many long hours delivering my cards to likely customers, scanning the *Women's Weekly* for the names of socialites, and sending them a business card.

When I arrived for work the first day, I was full of optimism and even said a prayer that all would go well. There was a knock at the door, but it wasn't a customer. It was a boy holding a beautiful bouquet of flowers. When I read the card, it was from my German friend, with all good wishes for my success.

On the first day I had several phone inquiries, and then my first client arrived in the afternoon. She told me that she was a magistrate. I gave her a fitting of the clothes she had bought recently at a local shop. She was very satisfied and I realised that the payment I had received paid my rent for the week. The rest would go towards expenses and profit. I kept a book in which I entered every transaction, although my charges were not exorbitant.

After the day's work, there was a short walk to the station, the usual half hour in the red rattler, then another walk of a mile from the station to our home.

After a quick cup of tea, there was the dinner to prepare for the family, which consisted of Joe, myself, Roberta and Bernard. Joe always helped with the washing up. Roberta would be off with a boyfriend and Bernard had his homework.

I was glad to hear that Joe had found some work in the plastics field. It was a night job, about 11pm until 7am. He had not shown any interest in my venture, and in fact never mentioned it. All my washing was done on a Saturday morning, while Joe did the shopping. I also cleaned the rooms thoroughly with the vacuum cleaner.

The business was going very well, and I began to work up quite a good clientele. I was able to put some money in the bank, and take a taxi home on rare occasions. Joe still demanded that I contribute to the expenses of the home, which I did. Of course, I should have charged him for all the washing, bed making, cleaning, cooking and gardening that I had to do, as he hated gardening.

Soon I found that I was getting more work than I could cope with. I decided to buy a large case, and bring any hems or easy jobs home and sit down after the evening meal and finish them off. Joe did not mind. He sat with his back to me every night, munching his peanuts, until it was time to go to work.

Before long it was imperative that I move to larger premises. I found just what I wanted in the fashionable Toorak area of Melbourne. This time it consisted of two large rooms on the ground floor. The first one was divided by a glass partition, making a waiting room. The other side was a mirrored fitting room, and at the back, completely on its own, was my workroom.

When I first started in the new area, I noticed that there were two other dress alteration businesses, but for some reason or another they soon closed down. The only one left was a men's tailor, to whom I would send any requests for male alterations.

I enjoyed every minute of my work and found it completely absorbing. Each client became a friend, and I met many wealthy people, some titled. The higher up their position, the more humble they appeared to be. I never had to advertise, as one client told another about me. I always informed them that I was expensive as soon as they came in the door, for the simple reason that I gave the best service, after years of experience.

One client told me that I had a reputation of being expensive but good.

A gentleman called one day. He presented a card, which showed that he was from the Labour and Industry Department. After inspecting the premises, he turned to me and said, "You are neither a factory nor a shop. You come under Home Industries, but if you ever employ anyone, let me know." Somehow for the next few years I managed completely on my own.

Joe, meanwhile, filled in his spare time listening to classical music, smoking and eating copious amounts of salted peanuts. His fits of anger and his shouting were still getting the better of him. One hot Sunday, I asked if he would take us down to the beach. He took us with great reluctance. In fact we nearly didn't arrive. Halfway there, I was bashed up and reduced to tears. In his anger he had managed to rock the car from side to side, intending to frighten us — not a wise thing to do while driving.

Joe pulled up at the side of the road and said he wouldn't continue until I had stopped blubbering (as he put it). When we finally arrived at the beach, we were told to go for a walk on our own while Joe sat inside, smoked, and read the newspaper. The crunch came when we arrived home and Joe turned to Bernard and said, "Bernard, you have my full permission to be rude to your mother."

I knew then that I would have to leave home. There was one thing preventing me at that time. Roberta had decided to get married to her boyfriend in the near future and had asked me to make her wedding gown.

It seemed at this time that Joe was a very disturbed man, and yet there was nothing that anyone could do. The doctor endeavoured to trap him into a visit by writing him a letter saying that he wished to discuss my health, but when Joe read the letter he tore it up, saying there was nothing wrong with me.

Roberta was duly married to the young man of her choice, the son of a local farmer. I had saved a little money and was able to give them a wedding breakfast at a delightful reception centre, not too far from the Catholic church where they were married.

After Roberta left home, Joe's abuse to me became intolerable. He had often screamed at me to get out. Then he would say that I would never leave because I hadn't the courage.

However, I decided that the time had come for me to take the plunge. I hated leaving Bernard, but I would be nearby if he needed me.

I had to be careful that Joe did not see me packing. If he did, there would have been more violence and he would have barred the way. I gathered my few belongings, placed them in three large suitcases, and ordered a taxi for nine o'clock the next day, which happened to be a bright Sunday morning.

Joe always slept late on Sundays, and because his room was at the back of the house he did not hear me leave.

I asked the driver to take me to my business premises in Toorak. I sat in the back with an immense feeling of relief. After a 30-minute drive, I unlocked the door of my new temporary home and took stock of the accommodation available. There was a well-sprung divan in the waiting room, a small kitchen at the back of the workroom, and even a small garden with a few evergreen bushes where I could sit on hot days. There was an electric jug in the kitchen and a toaster and plenty of power points everywhere.

The peace that I experienced was unbelievable. I had been told to get out so many times over the years, and I had threatened to leave on numerous occasions, but a sense of duty had prevented me from leaving earlier.

I had lunch at a small café up the road and went to evening Mass at a nearby church.

In the ensuing weeks, there were no phone calls from Joe or Bernard, no letters or signs of love. I felt that I had done the right thing after years of sadness. I missed Bernard, whom I loved very much, but I began to feel younger and at peace with the world. I was far too busy with my work to feel lonely.

The business improved so much that I was soon able to afford a two-bedroomed flat nearby, where I could live in a civilised manner and entertain my friends when I felt like it.

The time had come for Hans and I to part. We were both drifting on a sea of loneliness when we first met and had fallen deeply in love. Now, because he had a duty to his wife, who after a year had returned from Germany, it became apparent that I had to make the first move. It all ended very simply. No tears, just an empty gap, that we hoped time would heal.

The thought of death and an eternity spent in hell was the main criterion for my action, and of course I had wandered from the straight and narrow path of life and offended God, who was so good to me.

One evening after work, in trepidation I decided to return to the house to collect my oil painting of Roberta. It was one that I had taken some pains to complete a year before. I took the evening train, then hired a taxi to the house. I asked the taxi man to wait outside. I heard my husband say to Bernard, "Mum's come home." Then he disappeared. There were no welcoming arms, so I took the picture off the wall, placed it in a bag and returned to the station in the taxi.

It was getting dark, and I remember a gang of youths playing football on the platform. When the train came, I found a carriage as far away from them as possible, but to my surprise they raced down to my carriage. When I was seated I noticed that one had a knuckleduster in his hand, and another had a knife planted in his socks. There were about six people in the carriage. I wondered what I would do if I were attacked. At least I had the picture in a glass frame, with which I could retaliate. I admit that I was a little scared, but luckily nothing further happened.

Kevin had finished his time in the Royal Navy and was now living in Australia. He had announced his engagement to an English girl who lived in Australia. This would mean another meeting with Joe at the engagement party. On that occasion I noticed that Joe seemed very thin and sad. Then the wedding came along and I stood next to Joe again. I thought the memories of our own wedding might have some effect on him, but he seemed quite bereft of feeling.

I returned to my flat and to the business which kept me fully occupied eight hours a day. At weekends I would go to the nearest Bay resort with my friends. I used to take the bus, as Joe now had the car to himself.

On my way to the beach I used to pass some large houses and a block of flats. The thought occurred to me several times that if only in some way Joe could sell the house and pay back his debts, which were growing larger day by day, we could share a flat and perhaps have a peaceful retirement.

Joe always refused to sell the house. The debts that he had accumulated would have strangled both of us. It had also become known that he was leaving the house to Kevin.

To my mind there seemed only one thing to do, and one had to be cruel to be kind. I had to see a solicitor and force him to sell and pay back the debts. We were both almost due for retirement and wouldn't want to be burdened with debts at this stage of our lives.

It cost me 1000 dollars in solicitors' fees to reclaim my share of the house, the purchase of which had only been made possible from the money left to me in my mother's will. After all, my earnings had contributed to the upkeep of the family.

In England I had worked hard and had bought bedding and furniture out of my own pocket. I had even paid for the children's education.

The day came for the case to go to court. Joe was adamant to the last minute, but after constant conversations with the two solicitors he gave in, and the matter was settled out of court.

As soon as the business was finalised, we returned to the lawyer's office. Joe looked across at me and exclaimed loudly, "A fine wife you've turned out to be!" I said nothing, and walked out of the door.

As I walked out into the street, I turned and saw Joe standing on the footpath. He looked dazed, and his eyes followed until I turned the corner. I felt a pang of pity for him. The next day I rang him and told him of the two-bedroomed flat that I had in mind for him. I thought the sea air and some good food was all he needed to bring him back to health and strength.

He also needed to have his teeth out, as they were troubling him, and a new set of dentures was required.

Bernard decided to get married, so there would be just the two of us.

CHAPTER
THIRTY-TWO

The day Joe arrived at the flat, he could hardly walk up the stairs to the first floor, he was so weak. However, from that day on he made a remarkable recovery.

The flat was situated in the front of a block of four. The building was well constructed and surrounded by lawns. There was a balcony on which I grew some orchids.

There were ample carpets throughout the flat and I bought some new furniture and curtains.

Joe soon felt well enough to take a day job to fill in the time until his impending retirement.

He had suffered a mild form of diabetes for some time, and it was after drinking two cans of beer that he gave me the greatest shock of my life. He had gone to the bathroom to take a shower, when suddenly I heard a terrible crash. I ran to see what it was, but was able to open the bathroom door only slightly as Joe was lying on the floor, jammed between the bath and the door. He had crashed through the glass screen and a large chunk of glass was hanging over his body. One slight movement and it would have fallen on top of him. I couldn't move the door as he was blocking the way. My first inclination was to scream for help. I remember sitting on the bed saying, "Please help me, God."

I went back to the bathroom and somehow eased the door slowly open as Joe was beginning to come round. I

gently pushed the screen back, out of his way. He was
lying on his back. I quite expected his legs to be broken,
but he managed to get to his feet and I helped him onto
the bed.

In spite of this frightening episode, Joe began to enjoy
life, in his own way. He invented a word game which he
enjoyed playing with friends, and took walks down the
pier, just sitting in the sun and feeding the seagulls.

Until his retirement was due, he took a job as foreman
in a plastics factory to keep his mind occupied.

When eventually retirement came and we applied for
a pension, he turned his mind to founding a classical
recorded music society. The concerts were given
regularly every fortnight in a nearby church hall and
attracted a faithful group of music lovers.

Every detail was attended to with precision, and
programmes had to be selected and typed a week in
advance.

The old power of persuasion and gift of the gab
seemed to return, so that Joe was able to influence
celebrities to come and present programmes. This
always seemed to fill the hall to capacity.

On the opening night, the mayor was invited to say a
few words and declare the concert open. He was a little
plump man and sat with his wife. At Joe's beckoning, he
walked up on the stage and began to speak. I particularly
took stock of his well worn robes, the fur of which was
a little bit moth-eaten. Nonetheless he made quite an
impression. In the interval, a friend and I served tea and
biscuits. There was no charge to go into the hall, but a
collection was made at the interval. This usually covered

the cost of the hire of the hall. If only a few people came, we were out of pocket.

The succeeding weeks saw a progression of celebrities, the first being the British Consul, who said a few words in the interval and then left.

The next one was at my suggestion. I had heard some beautiful music on my transistor one night when I had retired to bed. I ran into the lounge, where Joe was engrossed in listening to a symphony concert. His earphones were perched on his head so as not to wake the neighbourhood. I made signs to him to listen. Reluctantly he removed the headphones and listened to the music.

It was by a French composer named Maurice Deruflé and was a Requiem. Next day, I suggested that Joe write to the composer, whom, I had learned by ringing the French Embassy, was still alive and living in Paris.

Joe wrote a letter and in due course received a reply in French, together with a card showing a picture of the famous church in Paris where the composer was organist for many years.

We decided to have a special presentation of the Requiem and to invite the French Consul to attend. The evening was a great success. Joe read out the letter from the composer and the hall was filled to capacity.

On other occasions Joe invited two well-known radio personalities, both attractive and well-spoken young women. They gave their time free in the cause of good music. He also inveigled the new young lady Mayoress to present a programme. On these occasions it was necessary for me to rush out and buy a bouquet of flowers, with which to present them after the programme.

Joe seemed so well now that I felt that I could be spared to take another sea trip.

I had invested the money from the sale of the house and there was some interest due, so I thought "Why not?" I was suffering from slightly high blood pressure from the past anxious years.

There was an advert in the newspaper for a cruise on a Russian ship named the *Michael Lermontov*. It mentioned all the places I had not seen, and had always wanted to go to. The route was via Honolulu, Vancouver, San Francisco, Los Angeles, Acapulco, Vila, Tahiti, Nuknaloafa and Auckland.

The cruise commenced from Sydney, so Joe drove me to the airport at Tullamarine for me to board the plane for Sydney.

The *Mikhail Lermontov* was a sleek 20,000-ton motor ship built in 1972 for the Baltic Shipping Company. On board there was a large ballroom, swimming pool and six bars, shops, beauty salon, a library and cinema. The ship was fully air-conditioned and equipped with stabilisers. The cost was a little over 1,000 dollars in 1978. Now the price for only a short cruise on another shipping line has doubled, and unfortunately no more Russian ships are allowed to sail from Sydney. The officers, crew, stewards and stewardesses were Russian, but the management staff were English and Australian.

I settled down in a comfortable cabin with three other ladies, one who was partly Maori and came from New Zealand and two Australians. The stewardess was a good-looking girl named Maria. She had been instructed not to converse with the passengers. She did her work efficiently and with a smile.

We sailed under Sydney Harbour Bridge at four o'clock in the afternoon and I began to revel in the gentle rolling of the ship as she trod the waves on her merry jaunt to faraway places. When the gong sounded for dinner, I was ready. It was refreshing to be able to wear some of the elegant clothes that I was unable to wear at home, simply because we never went out to dinner. Joe always said that he couldn't afford it.

I was placed at a table with three jolly Sydney women and two men from Brisbane. We all got on well from the start.

The menu was tastefully printed, and each cover decorated with a flower. On one side the menu was printed in French and the other side was in Russian. The names of the Captain, the Cruise Director, Chief Steward and Chef de Cuisine were printed in the centre of the folder. There was a choice of Russian or Continental food. Every meal was delicious and equal to that of the best hotel anywhere in the world. My charming young Russian waiter, sensing my sweet tooth, always saved me an extra pastry. It meant more time exercising on deck with the over-40s, but it was well worth it. One of the activities was a deportment class for the older women, which had amazing results.

The over-50s (and some were over 80), were asked to parade on the ballroom floor. They formed a circle and walked in time to the music. They were the usual sweet, unobtrusive, little old ladies, bosoms at half mast and walking with a stoop. Quickly the instructress came to the rescue.

"Come on dear," she'd say, "hoist up those bra straps." There was a pause while everyone was tugging at the offending halters. "Hold your tummy in, and walk as upright as you can."

The music played the usual cakewalk melody, "A pretty girl is like a melody". It was suggested that our hair be groomed for the final mannequin parade which would take place towards the end of the voyage.

What a surprise we received when we were finally treated to the mannequin parade. The little old ladies had become elegant elderly women. They all wore their most fashionable dresses, and it was a parade *par excellence*.

After calling at the sunny islands of Vila and Suva, we sailed in to Honolulu, where there was an exciting discovery tour each day for our two days ashore, ending with an evening spent at a night club and cabaret. The cabaret consisted of all varieties of Polynesian dances, enjoyed while eating a delicious smorgasbord. The next day was spent visiting Waikiki Beach, the very smart shops and the enormous shopping complex of Ohahu.

I was very surprised to see so many Japanese people living and working in Honolulu.

In the morning of the second day, we were being taken into the city on the coach when I noticed that Mass was just commencing at one of the older churches on the perimeter of the city. I informed the driver that I would find my own way back. The church was large and airy, every window and door opened wide, although the heat was not overpowering. All the people were dark-skinned, and the church was full to overflowing.

After Mass I began to look around for a taxi, but not one could be found, so I knocked on the presbytery door and a very kind priest ordered one for me. When it came, it was an enormous station wagon and cost me quite a few dollars, but it was worth every penny just to mix with those lovely people on that sunny Sunday morning.

The next long stretch of Pacific Ocean took us to Vancouver on the west coast of Canada. We visited the underground shopping area and saw beautiful spring flowers in bloom in Stanley Park. The air was clear and the sun shone as we gazed up at the high mountains, snow-capped, folding in tier upon tier as far as the eye could see.

After a two-day stop in Vancouver, we sailed down the west coast of America towards San Francisco.

During these evenings on board ship we were treated to entertainment of the highest quality, including a series of colourful Russian dances performed by the stewards and stewardesses. The bright and gaily embroidered dresses gained much applause from the passengers. The Russian lady who worked in the shop was an expert at playing the harp. The good-looking singer had been especially brought from the conservatoire of music in Leningrad. His deep baritone was a joy to listen to. Every item they performed reflected thousands of years of Russian culture.

I felt rather sad when our own entertainers brought some vulgarity into their act the next night.

We were soon approaching San Francisco. I was up on deck early to make sure that I did not miss the Golden Gate Bridge. How *could* anyone miss it? It is so enormous.

After the ship berthed, we were eager to go ashore and try out the trolley cars, which we did with gusto, and soon became lost in the busy shopping centre. Lunch was taken at Fisherman's Wharf. The second day was spent touring the environs of the city by coach, crossing and recrossing the Bridge. Chinatown provided us with another evening of fun.

It was after midnight when a coach drove us back to the ship. We were surprised to see a conglomeration of ambulances, fire engines, policemen and even the FBI, mingling with the passengers who were waiting to go aboard. There wasn't even a smell of smoke. Rumours were rife. The story going around was that a bomb had been attached to the propeller by some unknown hand. Hours later it was discovered that it was not a bomb at all, but a marker buoy that had become entangled in the propeller.

We were supposed to sail at midnight but were held up for a further two days, while a mysterious dome-shaped object was fixed to the forward deck. A warning notice was fixed in front of it, stating that it was dangerous to walk within two metres in front of it, because of radioactivity.

This gave way to further rumours that it was a satellite system that enabled the ship to send messages back to Russia.

Next day we were boarding the ship after a shore excursion, when a retired Catholic priest from New Zealand was going through the routine search for firearms. Each time he passed through the detector, the bell rang. It was obvious that there was some metal on his person. He took off all the metal that he could find, but the bell still rang. The contents of his pockets, his watch and even his trouser belt with its metal buckle were all removed. The American policeman standing by began to scratch his head, until it was realised that the old priest had a metal plate in his hip.

As soon as the new addition, the mysterious dome, had been added to the forward deck and the ship was clear to sail to Los Angeles, I went up to the ballroom after dinner to join my friends. I noticed the old priest sitting alone.

It was the common practice of the passengers to see who could reach the ballroom first and grab the most comfortable armchair. The priest always took a hard chair, while the Russian officers sat in a group nearby in comfortable armchairs.

Several times I left the group at my table to have a chat with him. He enjoyed a glass of beer or brandy and soda.

We watched the ballroom dancing, and he remarked to me that some of the wives were flirting with other men. Being the looker-on he saw most of the game. This proved to me that he was a humane and sensitive man, and his eyes were wide open.

One night after the cabaret, the New Zealanders had gathered together and were singing all the Maori songs in a corner of the ballroom. I realised that he was excited by the rhythmic war cries. He didn't need any encouragement to join the circle of his fellow countrymen and sing the songs with gusto. He knew all the words, and thoroughly enjoyed himself.

Later on he was to be of great help to the Russians. Being the only Catholic priest aboard, the Captain asked him if he would officiate at the burial at sea of a woman who died as the result of choking on a chicken bone. The woman had been operated on without success.

Two other people died from heart attacks, and the priest told me how glad he was to perform the funeral service when, in the early hours of the morning, those bodies were committed to the deep.

As the voyage was drawing to a close, he said that he would be glad to be home again in his retirement flat, with his sister to look after him.

The next port of call was Los Angeles, where we all went ashore at the dock nearest to the small town of San Pedro on the outskirts of Los Angeles.

The first day was to be spent touring Disneyland and the second day at Universal Studios.

The sky was milky grey with pollution, which soon gave way to hot sunshine and our luxury coach was soon speeding down the freeway. The driver turned off towards Long Beach, to give us a view of the *Queen Mary*, which was berthed at a nearby dock. Soon we were at the enormous car park outside the famous Disneyland. I was persuaded to sample most of the attractions, including the ghost train and the submarine.

Next day, we needed all our nervous energy to be able

to cope with all the jokes that Universal Studios had prepared to play on their guests.

A small tram was waiting to convey us through the leafy lanes and winding hills that are part of the enormous property owned by the Studios. We were amazed to see the water roll back on either side of us as we passed through what was once the set of the Red Sea in the famous Biblical film. It was a miracle of technology.

Our next fright was when we saw the artificial whale used in the film *Jaws*. It came bellowing out of the water, all its rubber blubber looking as artificial as it was not meant to be.

Further up the hill was a large tunnel, used in films where avalanches were required. The tunnel was lined with paintings of snowy mountains, which revolved at great speed while our little tram stood firm on the rails. The feeling was of being enveloped in snow and ice, and of the tram spinning round. It took me some time to regain my equilibrium. I was glad when we reached the top of the hill and I was able to buy some lunch and eat it in peaceful surroundings. The magnificent view of the San Fernando Valley unfolded in front of me.

We roamed around some of the larger studios and were treated to a show of performing dogs, and then rejoined our merry little tram which conveyed us back to the coach and thence to the ship.

Before going aboard there was just time to walk down the main street of San Pedro, a lovely Californian town where cowboys still swagger down the street wearing their ten gallon hats.

That night aboard ship I realised that my throat was red and raw, so I thought it a good idea to visit the ship's hospital. There was a Russian girl on duty, who did not speak English, so I pointed to my throat. She then indicated that I was too late and must come tomorrow. She suddenly had a change of mind, searched in a draw and produced a packet of tablets. The instructions were written on the box.

By the time we reached Acapulco I was feeling fine again. There was a kind of hush as the ship slowly approached Acapulco Bay. The sun was sinking behind the high mountains which grotesquely enfolded this luxury tourist resort. The taller buildings were tinged with a red glow, until finally all were dimmed and the coastline was lit by myriads of lights twinkling in the darkness. It was a magical moment as I stood on the forward deck, surrounded by people and yet alone with nature. There was a zephyr-like breeze playing on my cheeks, and the stillness of that night lives on in my memory. I was barely aware that my good-looking table tennis partner was standing behind me, whispering in my ear. I can't even remember his words. I was spellbound by that moment of beauty.

Next day we took the shore excursion to one of the largest hotels in the world. It was surrounded by a large golf course and boasted a Japanese garden complete with rivers and ornamental bridges, several swimming pools, and everything that money could buy. As we passed through the other end of town, we found women begging for money, and small children clinging to their skirts.

We watched the famous rock divers, risking their lives to entertain the tourists. These men dive into the sea from tremendous heights.

When we returned to the ship it was siesta time. A large truck was parked on the quay and, to my surprise, the driver had slung a hammock underneath the truck and was sound asleep.

The *Mikhail Lermontov* was soon making full speed ahead for Tahiti, on a homeward course. By this time the passengers were on friendly terms with each other, and were involved in deck games and parties. Even the serious Russian officers had begun to liven up a little.

A certain little plump woman at our table had, on entering the ballroom, grabbed an equally plump Russian officer and twirled him around to the rhythm of a lively waltz that was in progress. I wondered what the outcome would be. I think he enjoyed it, but soon regained his former dignity.

The seas were being kind to us. We had not had one bad storm since we left Australia, so that when we arrived in Tahiti we were all in great form, and ready for any eventuality.

It so happened that berthed ahead of us was a magnificent training ship of the Chilean Navy. Painted on her hull was the proud name *Esmeralda*. She was square-rigged and every part of her gleamed in the sunshine. The Tahitian scenery seemed to be enhanced by her presence.

My first efforts to go aboard were frustrated, because hundreds of Tahitians seemed to have the same idea. Then I caught sight of one of my friends from the

Russian ship, who was also keen to inspect this lovely vessel. However, we waited until the crowd had subsided and then made a fresh attempt to go aboard. This time we were rewarded, and an officer was delegated to show us around. The officer's name was Jorge, a young lieutenant and dressed impeccably in the white uniform of the Chilean Navy. He did not speak English, but fortunately my friend was fluent in several languages and therefore acted as my interpreter. After the tour of the ship, Jorge insisted that we join him for a drink in the beautifully panelled inner sanctum, the galley. He then disappeared and returned with a bottle which he described as the Chilean Navy's favourite drink. He proudly proclaimed the name of the drink — "Pisco". He uncorked the bottle and poured out a glass for each of us. We wished him good health, and my friend took a large gulp while I took a small sip. The taste was bitter, and not wanting to offend my friend I waited for an opportune moment to tip the glass into the nearest pot plant, of which there were several dotted around. It came when he went to search for a photograph of the ship as a memento of our visit. We were reluctant to leave our charming lieutenant, but the time had come to go ashore.

We spent the next morning sightseeing and the afternoon resting on the beach, but after tea my linguistical friend decided that she would like to take one of the local buses (which consisted of a truck decorated with native flowers) around the island. Since the ship sailed at midnight, I was dubious as to whether we would be back in time. In that case, she insisted, we

214

will go halfway and get a bus back. Inquiries were made, but no one seemed to have the time to give us a satisfactory answer to our question, so we joined the gaudily painted bus with the rest of the natives. When we had travelled about 15 kilometres, I began to feel uneasy, fearing that we would not be able to return without encircling the island. That would be too late, and the ship would have sailed without us. When the bus stopped at the next beach hotel, we alighted, entered the exotic garden, and were soon sitting under the palm trees, sipping a cool drink and watching the waves break on the sandy beach. But time and tide wait for no man.

It was soon time to go back to the stop and wait for the bus that my friend assured me would be coming to take us back to the ship. After an hour had passed, we became restless. I said to my friend, "The next car that comes this way, we must hail it. Otherwise we will not make it back to the ship."

Soon a small car appeared through the hotel gates and turned in the direction of Papeete. We waved. My friend explained the position to the driver, who happened to be French. She returned to me and said, "I put it to him so that he could not possibly refuse." Yes! He gallantly offered to take us to our destination. My friend chatted to him in French as we drove along the leafy Tahitian road. When we arrived, we thanked him, and offered to show him around the ship and buy him some Australian beer. It was imperative that we first get permission from the Chief Officer. That being done, we escorted our young and good-looking Frenchman on board to the nearest bar. It was amusing to watch the expressions on the faces of our fellow passengers and the subsequent questioning as to where we met him.

Our next few days were fully occupied with exercises on deck, lectures on Russian art and films of the magnificent paintings displayed in the Hermitage palace in Leningrad. One room on the ship was devoted to Marxist propaganda. Most of us sifted through it and drew our own conclusions.

Auckland, our next port of call, was a pleasant surprise, with its splendid shops and spectacular scenery.

The day after we sailed out of Auckland, the sky became dark and gloomy and we experienced our first storm. That night the ship tossed and shuddered, creaked and groaned. All doors leading to the decks were locked, as the sea washed over the struggling ship. Paper bags became evident in the corridors. Curiously my father's old remedy of boiled lemon sweets for *mal de mer* still held good, for I have never once been ill on any of my travels. However, it was a good time to play bingo, rather than watch the waves through the porthole.

After two days of stormy seas, we arrived back in Sydney. I spent a day sightseeing with friends, and then it was time to prepare for home.

The ship provided a variety of duty-free goods, made in Russia and very reasonably priced, so when I arrived in Melbourne I was not only laden with luggage, but also gifts for the family. There were two balalaikas for my sons, a Russian-style silver-grey fur fabric coat for Roberta, six flower-painted trays, a watch for my husband, and half a dozen classical records by well-known Russian composers. Heaven knows how I

216

managed to walk down the gangway with all these articles. It was lucky that Joe was at the airport to meet me. He was anxious to discuss his good news; the lady Mayoress had promised to present a programme.

I had to laugh when I looked in the appointment book. "Lady Mayoress comes to discuss programme. My conduct impeccable. Nuffink happened."

CHAPTER
THIRTY-THREE

Joe and I were quite on our own now, as Bernard, our youngest son, had married the girl he loved.

Having reached the age of 65, Joe applied for a pension and I gave up my dress alteration business in Toorak so that I could also apply for it, having reached 60.

From then on Joe's day began after 12 noon, the morning being spent lying in bed smoking numerous cigarettes, drinking copious cups of tea and eating chocolate biscuits, much against the doctor's orders. It had been discovered some years earlier that he had a mild form of diabetes, for which he was taking a daily pill.

The afternoon was spent typing out programmes for the fortnightly classical recorded music concerts. If I dared to interrupt, there would be a loud, vociferous explosion, and advice as to where I was to go. In spite of that, I used to insist that he have a walk in the afternoon for the sake of his health.

My thoughts were, "At last we will be able to relax together and enjoy the fresh sea air. Instead of my lone walks down the pier, I will have company." But it never quite worked out that way.

First of all, all the kitchen scraps were gathered into a bag, with which to feed the seagulls. Those birds, believe it or not, got to know him very well. When they saw him coming, one would raise the alarm, and a whole flock would wait on the roof of the milk bar, where he had gone to order the evening newspaper. I used to go on in advance and wait at our favourite seat. As soon as Joe emerged from the milk bar, they swooped down from all directions and followed him all the way until he disposed of the contents of the evil-smelling bag. On these occasions I found it necessary to wear a scarf on my head.

More often than not, Joe, being an inveterate talker, would spend a long time chatting to the milk bar proprietor's wife, a very attractive woman, so that I, growing tired of waiting, would have sauntered down the pier and back again before he reappeared.

My walks down the pier were often the lone affairs that I hoped to avoid. One day I asked him the reason for his dallying, and he replied that he didn't like walking with me because it always led to an argument. I couldn't remember ever having argued.

After dinner, Joe read the newspaper and watched television until midnight, when his real moments of happiness would begin. With earphones on his head, he would stay up until 2.30 a.m. listening to the classics. He played them so loud that, even with earphones, the sound reached the bedroom, and eventually I would have to rouse myself and remind him to come to bed.

The only cloud to darken our horizon that year of 1978 was one evening in September when the phone rang and Bernard told me that Roberta had been involved in a car accident. I rang the Alfred Hospital straight away. I was told that she was being operated on at midnight, and her little four-year-old girl was in the children's ward with a broken leg. Two other passengers were less seriously injured.

I prayed to God not to let her die. I rang the police and learned that a semi-trailer, turning a corner on the wrong side of the road, had crashed into them.

I knew there was nothing I could do that night but pray. Joe and I went to see her as soon as we were allowed to on the following afternoon, and also saw Jaqueline, with the broken leg.

It was a terrible shock to see our beautiful daughter with an oxygen tube in her nose, one leg covered in plaster and raised on a pulley. She had a plate in her leg and arm, and a large pin in her pelvic bone.

The ambulance man who treated her was at the bedside when we arrived. He described to us how she was carried out of the car unconscious after the "jaws of life" were used to get her out, and how he fought for three hours to bring her back to life with artificial respiration.

How can one thank such a dedicated man? These are our modern-day saints. All he would say was "It was my duty."

In my handbag was the bottle of water from the grotto at Lourdes, where Bernadette had seen the vision of Mary. I sprinkled the water over the damaged areas as inconspicuously as I possibly could and said a Hail Mary. I could tell that she was praying too.

Joe and I stood by and took turns to hold her hand. Somehow we knew that she would pull through. She had always been a courageous fighter.

It was not long before her daughter was taken from the children's ward and allowed to join her mother in the same room.

Joe and I cared for her other daughter, Kathrine, still in the nappy stage, until her father could organise help at home.

We visited her every day for the next six weeks, and noticed a remarkable improvement, until finally she was allowed to go home with the aid of a stick. Her husband managed to get help in the house. On hearing the news of her accident, he had grabbed his motor bike, rushed off to visit her in hospital, skidded on the wet road, fallen off the bike and fractured his knee.

After a spell at home, there was still to be a further stay at another hospital while Roberta had the plates removed from her arm and leg bones. The pin had been removed earlier from her pelvic bone.

When I look back to the Sunday prior to the accident, she had come to visit me with the children. We went for a walk to the sea front and were discussing the yoga group that she belonged to. I was not in favour of her joining the philosophy group, knowing that she was a practising Catholic.

I entreated her not to go to the next meeting, but with great self-assurance she reminded me that it was entirely her own business. She was right, of course, but if she had not gone to that meeting, there would not have been any accident. Maybe I had a premonition.

Joe meanwhile had become much thinner and was looking much older. His time was now taken up with presenting his programmes of classical music and inviting celebrities to present their own choice. He was never happier than to see his photograph in the local newspaper, gaining a little publicity for his concerts.

One morning he woke up and complained of a dull pain in his chest. "You must see a doctor," I insisted. He began to talk about dying, but that was not unusual, as often in a fit of depression he had mentioned death many times before.

"When I die," he said, "You won't cry, but Roberta will." I didn't help much by suggesting that I might be the first to go. I then sat beside him on the bed and kissed his cheek. He seemed embarrassed. It was not easy for him to show his feelings.

A visit to the doctor was arranged and x-rays were called for. It became obvious that there was a tumour on the lung.

Further arrangements were made for Joe to have a short period in hospital while various tests were made. I happened to be out when the doctor's secretary rang to make arrangements for Joe's visit. When I returned, Joe told me about the phone call, and to my amazement he had told the secretary, "Sorry, I can't come that day as I am presenting a programme." The tests were put off for another week and, of course, it gave the tumour time to spread to the rest of his body.

After the three days of tests in hospital, the results were such that Joe was told, in my presence, that he had three months to live or he could go any day in that period of time.

I remember Joe's reaction. It was one of anger. He blamed the doctor. The specialist informed me that this

222

was a natural reaction, and wrote on the form: "Shows Anger". I insisted on getting a taxi home, but Joe, stubborn as always, preferred the bus. It was very full, standing room only, but someone made room for him as he seemed so frail. I was glad when we arrived home.

When the day arrived for the next concert, Joe was as enthusiastic as ever. He had planned to present The Mass of St Cecilia by Gounod. Knowing that his strength was failing, he commissioned a friend to help him put out the chairs, while he made all the other preparations for the evening.

With the help of his friend the Presbyterian Minister, Joe made the evening as perfect as he could for the few faithful friends who attended. Everything was carried out with Army precision.

When he arrived home, he said firmly, "That is the last concert that I shall give." Next day, he took to his bed and spent only a short time listening to music in the evening.

A day later we received a visit from our landlord. We had always regarded him as a friend, but he broke the news that he had increased the rent by 20 dollars a week, which was quite beyond our means. God came to our aid very quickly through a kind neighbour, who, on hearing of our predicament, told me of a flat that had become vacant in the same road.

Arrangements were made to move within the next few days. Joe was still able to walk short distances, so I suggested that he have a look at the new flat. I held his arm and led him up the road to the flat, and he agreed that it would be suitable. He became very breathless on the way home and went straight to bed.

Two days later the removal men arrived at eight a.m. My problem now was how to move a dying man to a new flat and attend to the positioning of the furniture and so on. I need not have worried, as my lovely daughter and her capable husband came to the rescue.

Joe remained in bed until all the furniture had been taken out, then put on his dressing gown and Roberta helped him into her car and drove him up to the flat, where there was a chair for him to sit on. She then produced a lunch of chicken and salad. The removal men had gone for their lunch, so we waited until they returned. My afternoon was fully occupied with attending to Joe and making sure he was comfortable, and cleaning out the old flat and then returning to supervise again.

The doctor came the next day and prescribed painkillers for Joe, who was beginning to ask for them when the pain became unbearable. He slept in the single bed next to mine. I seemed to spend the night listening to his breathing and wondering if he would suddenly stop. I had the phone numbers of the ambulance and the doctor handy. All relatives in England had been contacted. One brother, a Catholic priest, phoned from England, but I felt that it would be too late for him to make the long journey. The last concert had been on 15th November. It was now 15th December, 1981.

A bed had been booked at the Bethlehem Hospital, only a short drive from our flat. Strangely enough, the hospital was run by the Catholic Community of Sisters called the Little Company Of Mary.

I wanted to look after Joe as long as possible, but events during the night made me wonder if I should call the ambulance. First of all he insisted that I pull down the blind, and pointed at the wall where no blind existed. I pretended to do so, but he became angry and threatened me. Then he insisted on going to the bathroom on his own. I jumped out of bed to help him, but he pushed me away, saying that be could manage quite well. I waited for him to reurn. The door opened and he took the wrong turning towards the glass panelled front door and collapsed in a heap on the floor. I tried to help him up; he still seemed conscious, but I could not lift him. His nose was bleeding profusely as he had knocked it on the corner of the kitchen door. Worst of all, I could not open the front door because he was in the way. I wanted to call a neighbour. Failing that, I picked up the phone and dialled the local police station.

In five minutes two kindly young policemen were on the doorstep. They managed to ease the door open slightly and lift Joe back to bed. I thanked them and then called the doctor. The result was there were no bones broken.

The next day, arrangements were made for a nurse to come and help him, but when Joe saw this glamorous young nurse standing beside him I think he thought he was already in Heaven.

"Where did you come from?" he asked.

"I've come to rub your backside," she replied.

"You are very beautiful. You've made my day."

Joe was taking nourishing drinks but could not eat anything except small pieces of toast. When he told me he could no longer bear the pain, I would give him the pills that the doctor had ordered, and then he would relax. "Come here. I want to tell you something," he would say. I obediently sat on the edge of the bed, held his hand and kissed his cheek. The words never came, and we sat silently for a few minutes.

I felt that the time had come for Joe to go into the care of the nuns, where he would get more professional attention. The social worker at the hospital where he had had his tests agreed with me, so I rang for the ambulance. When it arrived Joe refused point blank to go into it. The men waited 20 minutes, then had to go on to another job.

The following day the Catholic priest came and gave him the last sacraments of the Church. Joe seemed more at peace, but the pains in his lung and back were becoming more intense.

Once again the pretty young social worker came to try and persuade Joe to go in the ambulance, but without success. It was a repetition of the day before.

I somehow managed to dash out on my bicycle to buy the necessary groceries, leaving the front door open and hoping that things would be all right. When I returned home, Joe informed me that he wanted a shower. I said that it would be better if I gave him a blanket bath. I had in my youth taken a course in home nursing and had received a certificate for it. "No!" Joe insisted on taking a shower. My heart was in my mouth as his frail body stumbled towards the bathroom. I turned on the shower and washed him down as best I could. He slumped down on the chair, his whole body blue as I rubbed him vigorously. He let me guide him back to bed, where I gave him a warm milk drink. He then asked for his electric razor. When I returned from cleaning up the bathroom, I received a shock. His face was covered in blood as he had gone over all the lumps and bumps. I wiped his face and put antiseptic cream on it.

Joe had now developed a habit of lying on the side of the bed, and I was fearful that he would fall out onto the floor.

Once again I contacted the welfare worker at the hospital. This time she said she would take him personally to the Bethlehem Hospital in her own car. Since he was usually influenced by a pretty face, and she was a charming, intelligent young lady, I hoped that she would do the trick.

My prayers were answered. He fell for her charm, and between the two of us, one each side, we managed to support him to the door, where the car, a large station wagon, was ready to take him. He sat next to her in the front seat. I placed a blanket around him. I think he thought he was going for a joy ride, as when we arrived at the hospital he seemed confused, but the nuns were there to administer to him. He was then placed in a large cot, from which he could not fall out. While this was being done I was shown into a waiting room opposite.

He was protesting very loudly, and the nuns were using firm but kindly tactics. I heard him shout, "Where's my wife?" I opened the door to speak to him, but he had already received a tranquilliser. I went home to have the first night's sleep for many weeks and with my renewed energy intended to visit him the next day. I was preparing to visit him when the phone rang at about midday. The sister in charge suggested that I come at once. Our two sons and their wives had been summoned, also our daughter and her husband.

It was Christmas Eve, 1981, just a month after his last concert. The family were all gathered around the bed. Joe lay still, his eyes closed, his breathing laboured. The sister in charge gave me courage by just being near. We knelt down by the bed and said the Rosary. Before we had finished, sister rose and took the oxygen tube from his nose. She said, "He is now in God's care."

My daughter was crying, but, for me, no tears came as I watched him breathe his last, and I let out an agonising groan.

Joe's faithful friend, the Presbyterian Minister, who had been present all the time, offered to take me home. I experienced a great sense of peace and slept that night. The next day was Christmas Day, which I spent with the grandchildren. Somehow I managed to find them a few small gifts. Their happy faces gave me new courage. My four-year-old grandson Kristen had the answer when told that Grandpa had died. He said, "Don't worry, Grandma. He's gone home."

ISIS publish a wide range of books in large print, from fiction to biography. A full list of titles is available free of charge from the address below. Alternatively, contact your local library for details of their collection of ISIS large print books.

Details of ISIS complete and unabridged audio books are also available.

Any suggestions for books you would like to see in large print or audio are always welcome.

7 Centremead
Osney Mead
Oxford OX2 0ES
(01865) 250333